I WISH
I'D
KNOWN

10 Ways to Break Ancestral Patterns,
Free Yourself from the Past,
and Manifest Your Dreams

SARAH VIE

Printed in the United States of America

Hardcover ISBN: 978-1958714263
Paperback ISBN: 978-1958714270
Ebook ISBN: 978-1958714287

Library of Congress Control Number: 2022945205

CHICAGO · NEW YORK · PARIS · ROME
Muse Literary
3319 N. Cicero Avenue
Chicago IL 60641-9998

To myself who has weathered all the storms.
To my children who have witnessed my transformation.
With all my heart, I love you all.

Contents

Foreword

Dear Beautiful Soul,

I wrote this book just for you because I was in the same place you are now when I began exploring another version of myself.

As a result of my journey, I feel as if I have given birth to another baby. I have been rebirthed into myself, or perhaps I reparented my little girl self by using the tools you will uncover as you read each chapter. Everything I share with you in the following pages are tools I have used to unearth and heal from my own past.

The old roots of who I thought I was are now replaced with my truth. I have ascended and blossomed into the woman I knew I could be. This journey has been one of the most difficult paths to uncover, but I would never have experienced it any differently.

You are in for a beautiful ride, and on the other side you will discover a part of you that is more powerful than you ever could have imagined. If I did it, so can you!

Pure love to you,
Sarah Vie

Chapter 1

My Reason for Healing

Who I Was vs. Who I Had to Be

Most children want to live their lives free from expectations, responsibilities, and living the life their parents wish they had lived. Sometimes our parents have a different plan for us. The unfulfilled lives of our parents are played out in hopes of recreating what was once lost.

My earliest memory of myself is at age five. These memories are vague, but I get a sense of who I was by a little photograph I have always carried with me. That memory has followed me everywhere for the past five years as I began to examine myself on the inside.

In my personal healing journey, I lovingly remember the little girl with a dirty blonde pixie haircut. She wore her handsewn gingham plaid shirt made by her mother who was very talented at sewing clothes. That special shirt was only worn for class pictures. It was with great excitement she lay out her little outfit the night before, carefully smoothing out the wrinkled fabric in preparation for the next day at her beloved school, East Bradford. In the little cherished photo, a soft peaceful smile mirrored her innocence. This picture reflects my original essence.

I was that little girl playing with her brother who promised him, "Let's not fight today," and each and every day we ended up in our rooms separated from yet another fight. It was a good intention.

Some of my fondest memories were always playing outside. It was that time when our parents sent us out the door in the morning and we wouldn't return until dinnertime. There was not the distraction of social media or watching endless episodes of *Friends*.

One of my favorite memories was ice skating on cold, winter days with a thermos full of hot chocolate, which was normally opened before we even began. The sweet taste of chocolate was something I couldn't resist. Sometimes my mom would indulge us with a few sugary marshmallows. Treats like that were a rarity but much appreciated when they were discovered.

I can remember the small pond we would visit with our backpacks full of belongings for our day out together. To a small child this pond was massive, but in actual fact, it was an overflow of a small creek dammed up from debris floating downstream. It felt much bigger to my little eyes. My brother and I found joy in this and were entertained for hours. It confirms that children need so very little to feel happy.

Another fond memory with my brother was making tree forts and taking old blankets and sheets to create a comfortable space to sleep. We would crawl up the steep bank where glorious, old trees stood with dark hollows in their trunks. We would attempt to start the night sleeping in our newly renovated fort with our pillows and blankets, only to return inside when an incessant amount of creepy crawlers found their way into our sleeping bags. Upon this discovery, I remember dragging our pillows and blankets down the banks covered in honeysuckle, across the driveway in the dark, back into our old stone house. Named the "Honeymoon Cottage," our house dated back to 1717. This lovely, small home with thick stone walls offered our family a climate inside that only we experienced—we turned up the heat by putting on another sweater. Our enormous fireplace with the crackling fire in the living room was a source of heat we always appreciated.

The years playing with my brother were when I remember truly being a child without a care in the world. The sticks in my hair and the mud on my cheeks are memories I hold dear in my heart. These memories reflect the creative, fun-loving little girl who yearned to play and just *be*. The opportunity to be that little girl who had other dreams of what she wanted to do when she grew up, all seemed to disappear. It wasn't until later in life my true purpose was revealed when I began my spiritual journey within.

My intention of this first chapter is not to disrespect how my parents brought me up. They were loving, generous people who always had positive intentions for the three of us. Rather, I give you a glimpse into why I felt so unhappy and uncomfortable with myself for most of my life. The impact was on the decisions and choices I made when I was an adult.

Being a parent of four grown children, I understand how difficult it is to parent in a healthy and loving way without making a lot of mistakes.

Believe me, I made my mistakes with my own children, but for some reason I was always conscious about not continuing the same pattern I experienced as a child.

I can remember becoming aware of that similar pattern I grew up with one day when I was teaching my son, Avery, to ride. In my mind he had the worst posture and I reminded him that he looked like a "sack of potatoes," which was something said to me during my riding instruction. At that very moment, he dismounted and said, "I don't want to ride anymore, Mommy." That moment changed the course of patterning with my children. Instead of riding, he turned his passion into music, and I will share more details in the pages to come.

Raising my children was the first time I began taking a closer look at myself and how I was raised. I didn't understand back then why I felt so uncomfortable in my own skin or why I felt energetically unsettled and out of alignment.

Our parents do the best job they know how, and I honor that. No parent sets off on their journey with the idea they will bring pain to their children. All of us parents have a positive intention as we begin the unchartered and unknown waters of parenthood. I lived a happy life with no physical abuse, and my basic needs were always met. But I did live with the pain and trauma my parents experienced from which they never healed. It was thought of in those days as a weakness to show emotion and to explore the depths of yourself.

In this chapter, I share my story of healing. I will explain to you what happens in each generation that creates those old patterns we hold on to in our genetic DNA. This is my purpose in life and was revealed to me after "clearing" out my old beliefs and identities that did not belong to me. Instead, what has been revealed to me is the person I was born to be, the spirit that was calling me, but I wasn't listening.

I only began horse riding because that is what I was told to do. It was not a burning desire of mine, unlike my mother who loved horses so much she would gallop on all fours pretending to be a horse when she was young. Being born and raised in England, she enjoyed horses, which seemed to be a part of the culture. She had aspired to be a steeplechase jockey, which quickly became an unfulfilled dream. Riding horses became my life at the tender age of four. I knew nothing else.

The Healing Memory

It was another early morning and time to get up before the sun rose, clean my tack, feed my horse, and make sure I had everything ready for another riding competition. What I really wanted to do was to be invited to my friend's house for an overnight sleepover, stay up really late eating junk food, and talk about boys. Instead, my boots were polished, my shirt ironed, and my spurs, riding crop, and britches were all ready for the day ahead.

I remember the excruciating nerves my body would begin to feel the evening before and the morning of each competition. The knot deeply embedded in my gut seemed like a part of me. I was not afraid of the actual competition but afraid of making another mistake—having my mother be disappointed in my talents and embarrassing her friends and my very expensive English riding trainer. Looking back, this feeling of my stomach churning turned into crippling performance anxiety.

My mother and I drove as we always did, with the horse trailer hitched behind our faithful family station wagon. The car witnessed my growing from a little girl into an older young lady who didn't believe in herself.

One day in particular, after driving quite a long distance, we rounded the final corner and turned onto the tree-lined driveway to the competition's grounds. I began pulling my hair neatly into my hair net and carefully tucking my long braids under my black velvet helmet. I noticed the nerves bubbling up as I knew it was time to shine.

For three days I competed in three different phases of the competition. The first day was dressage: the quiet perfection of obedience, flexibility, and balance between the horse and rider. Day two was all about endurance and speed, jumping over twenty large obstacles at a perfectly timed fast speed. The final day was jumping precision in a controlled manner, jumping over a variety of obstacles in an enclosed ring. After three days the score was accumulated, and the competitor with the lowest score would triumphantly walk away with the victory.

Dressage was my strongest event. The quiet fluidity of my horse connecting to me at every turn seemed to come easy to me. My beautiful black mare, Imari, performed all stages of the dressage test with ease and precision. After the eight-minute performance, our score was outstanding, and we led the rest of the pack of talented young riders after the first day. I remember my mom almost floating on air knowing my horse performed so well.

Day two was cross country and endurance. This day was not my favorite. Unearthed emotions came to the surface like a violent volcano about to erupt. The most challenging aspect of this phase was making sure not to take a wrong turn or jump too fast. The slightest misjudgment could affect my accumulated score. I remember I began my cross country with great enthusiasm, thinking positive thoughts as I listened to the countdown begin. 10, 9, 8, 7, 6, 5, 4, 3, 2, 1, Go…

My horse's breath rhythmically mirrored her thundering hooves as we cleared fence number one with ease. We galloped on to the next obstacle. I can still remember rounding the turn into the second fence with too much speed. In that split second, as I turned into the four-foot upright fence, I heard a loud cracking sound as my horse's front legs hit the top rail. I can still remember tumbling and my horse's weight hitting the ground with tremendous force. I looked up, searching the crowd for my mom who stood behind the ropes with my trainer. It was at that moment I knew I had disappointed my mom again, as I saw her and my trainer shaking their heads instead of running to see if I was injured, which would have shown they cared about me. Instead of taking care of myself, after witnessing her familiar reaction, I got back on my horse to continue in hopes I could possibly regain my dignity and make my mother proud of my effort.

There were at least eighteen more jumps to complete. As I galloped on to the next fence, fear suddenly took over my entire body—not the fear of the jumps, but the fear of facing my mother's disappointment yet again. I had "messed up" another opportunity to be seen as that little girl, rather than someone who had "failed" to gain validation from her mom and feel loved. I galloped on until I could see the next fence that stood over the crest of the hill.

The fear became too much for me. At that moment, a plan began churning in my head that I would fall off my horse again, pretending to faint. *Yes, that is good. This will be my excuse for not continuing.* This would not only get me validation, but attention. I would feel seen and loved, finally. Yes, this was a great plan, so this is what I did. As my horse approached fence number three, I dropped the leather reins, took my boots out of the stirrups, and pretended to fall gracefully off my horse and faint, as if I had a concussion from the great fall at fence number two.

I remember the entire episode as if it were yesterday—the ambulance, the medics talking with concern, the stretcher they loaded me on, the siren as the ambulance left the grounds, the blood pressure machine checking my vitals. I even remember half opening my eyes when the medics weren't looking and smiling to myself as I had just experienced my own great escape.

Arriving at the hospital, I was quickly taken to a private room. I was checked and rechecked for signs of a concussed state, broken bones, or anything that would help the doctors make an assessment of my impending condition. They couldn't find anything.

After a few hours of treating myself to free hospital food and afternoon television, it was time to act again. I heard the familiar English voice of my mom in the hallway before she walked into the room with that stoic and unemotional look on her face. This was my cue to continue this charade of physical brokenness. I pretended to slowly open my eyes, pulled the bed sheet up to my chin, and grimaced as if in pain. I was so good.

Her words would be my healing. There was that familiar phrase I had heard before. She said, "What is wrong with you, you have a perfectly good horse!" There it was again—that small phrase I kept believing in, the phrase that stopped me from thinking I could do anything, and the phrase that became my identity. There was something wrong with me.

In my heart I believed there was something wrong with the little girl who wanted to play with her brother and laugh and sing in the rain; to have sleepovers and stay up way too late and who wanted to imagine and dream of what to be when she grew up. I desperately wanted to reignite my inner sparkle, but I didn't know how. There was something wrong with me, and I believed that for most of my life. Healing has been the work of this inner journey.

After a few years of practicing and repeating many of the same failure patterns, I finally won one of the most prestigious competitions of my unwanted riding experience. However, the victory was tainted by more words that convinced me I would never be good enough, ever. I cannot exactly remember my age, so I am going to say I was sixteen. I had trained hard with my Olympic horse trainer, after being sent away for the summer to be a working student. In exchange for extensive instruction, I would have to clean ten stalls each morning, feed and water all the horses, and then be ready at 8 a.m. sharp for my instruction. I still to this day have dreams that I am running late, and I can't make my legs move.

This was some serious riding. I had to make the most of what was given to me, I was told. There were no mistakes that would be accepted. My summer was preparing me for the competition to be held in October in the countryside of Middleburg, Virginia, the land of horses and really nothing else. Fields and fields of green grass and dozens and dozens of perfectly groomed horses filled the beautifully manicured paddocks.

I can remember the day of my competition. My horse was transported from Maryland, where my trainer lived, to Virginia, where the competition would be held, in a very fancy horse transport unlike my old trailer with paint patches to cover the impending rust spots. My mom had arrived in another vehicle, so we didn't have the traditional drive together that I was used to.

I competed in each competition with great skill and precision. The final day, I had been leading by only a few points. The fences were set, and I waited patiently until the announcer called my name to enter the final phase of the three days: "And our next competitor is Sarah Smith riding Imari." Off I went. I remember the familiar noise of my horse's hooves as she cantered rhythmically to each fence, feeling the signals sent through the leather reins.

The round of jumps seemed to come to me with great ease, rounding each corner with impeccable precision. It was as if my horse and I were one. The last three jumps were all I had to complete without any rails knocked down. The last line of jumps was a triple combination. Knocking down one rail would put me out of contention. The first jump Imari cleared . . . two strides and a second one cleared . . . two strides and her front hoof rattled the top rail, but it managed to stay put, and I galloped across the finish line. My mind was a blur filled with joy that finally I would feel validated by my achievement and feel loved.

Imari's coat streamed with sweat from her physical effort. I dismounted and went to search for my mom. At first I couldn't find her, but when I saw that earth-green raincoat and those practical Wellington boots she always wore, I knew we would be in great celebration of this momentous achievement. Her back was turned away from me as I approached. She heard my screams of celebration, and she slowly turned toward me with that emotionless expression. I felt a sinking in my stomach. Instead of that congratulatory hug, I heard more words that confirmed the belief I was not good enough no matter what I did, even when I won.

She turned her head, and her words stung like a miserable hornet: "Okay, okay, Sarah. It's not that great, settle down." I felt deep confusion, not understanding her verbal intention. What I can piece together was that underneath this intention, she had pride in me, but she was not able to express it.

Yes, this was my interpretation of her words. What I didn't know then was she had experienced the lineage of her family. Her father valued her only by her achievements. He treated her like a servant, comparing her to her army hero brother. Nothing she ever did was good enough.

As a child, my memory of my grandfather was filled with pure terror. When I was about six, I can remember, he demanded I sit on his lap to read to me. He would confuse two children's stories as he began to turn the pages. The smell of tobacco smoke reeked on his English tweed jacket. On occasion, he would place his lit pipe in his pocket only to find his pocket smoldering and catching on fire. I remember when I didn't laugh at the confused stories, he would banish me from his lap and out of the room. I felt so afraid when he slowly shuffled into the room each morning to drink his morning cup of tea, served by my grandmother. Even the walls of their fifteenth century English cottage seemed to hold its breath.

I wish I had known what I know now. If I had unearthed these cemented ancestral beliefs, it wouldn't have taken me a lifetime to heal.

Chapter 2

Just the Facts

I am not a scientist filled with facts about healing. I am a woman who has been dedicated to finding her own path on her life journey and becoming connected to the original essence she was born to be. I have come to this place of discovery by exploring energetic healing, practicing the art of meditation, and studying with countless emotional and spiritual mentors throughout my life. I have not traveled this road alone.

Rebuilding and transforming myself, honestly, hasn't been an easy road, but has been the most enlightening experience I have ever lived through. I have been determined to rewire my old identity that didn't even belong to me and to energetically step into the person I knew I was.

Gone are the old stories I thought defined me. Gone is the fear that crippled me from living my purpose. Gone is a closed heart that couldn't receive love. Gone is the old language I spoke to myself that imprisoned me in the place of limitations. Fear was the only thing that held me back from the exploration of going within.

What I still know is that this healing journey won't end until I take my final breath. I am completely committed to deepening the relationship with myself.

Those words spoken by Gandhi, "Be the change that you wish to see in the world," are almost impossible when we haven't healed our own pain. We mirror our inner pain and trauma to not only people closest to us, but also to the outer world. When we react in anger to someone cutting us off in traffic or when we become impatient in a grocery line. When we react to a person in front of us aimlessly placing her items on the conveyor and discussing her latest trip to the Bahamas, we come from a place of unresolved pain. Is standing in line waiting really stressful or is it our interpretation of the situation?

When we "google" the word "healing" there are dozens of different meanings associated with this little word: bringing to an end or conclusion, to make healthy, whole or sound, getting well, mending, just to name a few.

Healing is a personal journey for each of us. One hundred percent of all people in this world have had some sort of trauma or pain they encountered as a child. Even when someone says, "I had a perfect childhood," we can understand that underneath those words is an unresolved issue that doesn't want to be examined. My unresolved issue turned into a closet full of clothes. These clothes were ways to *fill my emptiness.*

Before I took time to examine my underlying issue of trauma, I used shopping to numb out my healing. I did not need nor truly want what I was buying, but the temporary elated sensation seemed to be worth every maxed-out credit card and story I told my then husband when I took yet another bag in the house. I would go as far as hiding those bags in a room until he wasn't looking. I never really wore the clothes. They hung in my closet to reflect a sense of security and the false idea that I had nothing to heal, an old friend that made me feel secure and would be waiting for me to revisit whenever I needed. The deepening into myself could wait one more day.

The behavior was easier for me to see in others than it was to see in myself. I saw this behavior in a dear friend of mine. I would witness her behavior when we would shop together. When she couldn't decide on one expensive piece of jewelry, she would buy two. She then ended up borrowing money from friends and family in order to pay for her bills. I offer this example without any judgment, but with a curiosity of how we stuff the feelings of uncomfortable emotions with things on the outside of us.

What is Trauma and Why Do We Need to Heal It?

Trauma is an emotional response to an event, such as an accident, assault, or natural disaster. Often, the level of internal trauma is just too frightening to acknowledge, so we push it down and ignore it in hopes it will just miraculously disappear. The emotional pain is something we either feel, heal, and let go or it becomes something we experience over and over again. These unhealed experiences somehow calcify our identity, which is based on many factors. The internalization of parental values and our childhood culture can be an imprint to our identity. One of the main ways we identify ourselves is with this perception of our past. Our past usually does not belong to our esoteric self, or the self we were born with.

Trauma does not have to be physical abuse, sexual abuse, or witnessing a death. To a young child, trauma can be experienced in many different ways—feeling left out, not being seen or heard, and not feeling like enough can be as traumatic as an unwanted slap or inappropriate sexual contact. Both have an impact that can be very damaging. Negative words and name calling used by an elder or a sibling can "break your bones." Do you remember when someone would say, "Sticks and stones may break my bones but words will never hurt me"?

According to Harvard University psychiatrists in the Harvard Mental Health Letter, scolding, swearing, yelling, blaming, insulting, threatening, ridiculing, demeaning, and criticizing can be as harmful as physical abuse, sexual abuse outside the home, or witnessing physical abuse at home.

I remember being teased on the bus as an eight-year-old. The bright yellow school bus that picked me up each morning became a place of deep dread. I remember sitting in the front seat in hopes of being invisible to the bullies who called me names until I cried. I will detail this story in the next few chapters. Words can be traumatizing and painful and can leave scars that take a lifetime to heal. The individual interpretation of pain becomes the distorted identity we carry from childhood to adulthood.

In reality, trauma comes in many forms and is responsible for how we feel internally. This internal vibration creates our negative emotions or can create our daily thoughts.

I also see this reality over and over again in my coaching. The patterns are different, but the remedy can be similar. I find it fascinating how my clients have grown up completely differently but come to me in the same place of healing. Their childhood pasts are different, but the beliefs in themselves are limited and misaligned.

Healing from those old stories that created the false identity can be challenging. The beginning of the journey is frightening, but once we set our intention to begin, the hill we get to climb seems possible. I always say, "It's better to do a little something, than nothing at all."

The Symptoms

Weight gain, over-shopping, drinking too much, obsession with negative thoughts, or staying in abusive relationships are some of the many symptoms that tell us something within us is out of alignment. We then create a solution to conceal the uncomfortable, energetic sensation in our body. I call them empty fillers that turn into lifelong habits that will never fulfill us in a satisfying way. We aren't born with limitations about ourselves: I hate my body, I am not enough, I can't do that. These beliefs are learned from society or modeled from our family of origin. The only two things babies are afraid of are being dropped and loud noises. Everything else is inherited.

When patterns come up, instead of sitting with it, feeling it, and understanding the story or emotion, we immediately want to relieve that discomfort and search for something instantaneous. That instant relief, of course, is temporary, but we believe we have cured ourselves, until we notice that pattern showing up again and again and again.

In my coaching, I witness the concealed emotions in relationships. I listen to my clients' disappointment after entering a new and loving partnership. The ecstasy of newness is replaced by similar name calling and abuse. When they are unwilling to heal the pain, the pain shows up in a similar way.

Our society seems to encourage healing by material things such as cars, houses, jewelry, and designer clothes. We are not encouraged, nor taught, to heal ourselves. We are only taught to ignore what wants to come through, and we reach for a quick fix. If we have material things and look a certain way, we show up to the world as if we have nothing to heal. The perfect images on Instagram or on our social media platforms become the identity we want others to see.

Trauma Did Not Begin with You . . .

According to a scientific study by Dr. Rachel Yehuda, director of Mount Sinai's traumatic stress studies division, children can hold on energetically to three generations of unhealed pain and trauma in their DNA. Pain and trauma can be a part of our lives even when we haven't lived with physical or emotional abuse.

Take for example one of my beautiful clients who noticed he was experiencing unhappiness that he had never experienced before. He firmly stated that he had had a perfect childhood: adoring parents, private education, and all his needs met in amazing ways. He kept asking me, "What is wrong with me and why am I feeling so out of my natural happy alignment?" Unhappiness was showing up in his life in his intimate relationships, and he wasn't sure why. I asked him what he noticed in his patterns. He mentioned he didn't like how critical he was to his wife. Specifically, he felt he was only noticing the things his wife did wrong.

Leaving dishes in the sink sent him into a physical rage he couldn't explain nor control. He noticed that if any of his family members did not put things away in the exact order they were found, his reaction was beyond unhealthy. Setting the table was an ordeal, he remembered. He even went as far as measuring the distance of the knife and fork placement before anyone sat at the table. This turned into an obsession he couldn't explain.

Deep into our work together, I began unearthing the family traits of his parents. Upon closer examination, I learned his grandmother and mother both experienced being prisoners of a war camp in Indonesia. He offered a story to me about how his grandmother and mother were only allowed one or two personal items when they were taken away from their homes so many years ago. The small trinket his mother cherished was a little doll her father had given her for her birthday. The sweet doll with tangled hair and a bright red smock became something she held on to for comfort. The fear of losing what belonged to them birthed the angst that was passed on to their next generation, unleashing this fear of control onto his beloved family. What he didn't understand was that he was carrying a trauma from his ancestry.

Another client of mine has been working hard to release the crippling fear of rejection. She had been noticing that she would begin to beat herself up or work harder to find her value when she heard any harsh comments at her work or in her relationships. Her perceived rejection was taking hold of her, and she began the spiral into self-judgment. The inner narrative began with repetitive name calling toward herself. After our work together, she understands it didn't begin with her. In her morning meditation she uncovered a revelation. She shared with me that her grandmother was given away/stolen from her parents at the age of six. After the first world war, her parents sent her from Hungary to the Netherlands for a six-month recovery period. Her Dutch foster parents never gave her back and hid letters from her father, begging them for her return. This left her grandmother thinking that her parents didn't care about her anymore. Susan's mother was born in the last winter of the second world war when people were starving, and she was the unexpected twin her grandmother had no idea she was carrying. Her mother was born and lived the rest of her life in the shadow of her twin sister.

This is powerful evidence of where our pain and trauma can be seeded. This then begins the thread of what needs to be healed.

Pain and trauma can be a part of our lives even when we haven't lived with physical or emotional abuse. Our pain cannot only show up in our relationships, but in any area of our lives, from excess weight we hold on to, to the relationship we have toward money, or to how we take care of ourselves and our health.

Even if we haven't directly been affected, we can experience symptoms without having any of the original trauma.

It Didn't Start with You: How Inherited Family Trauma Shapes Who We Are and How to End the Cycle is an eloquently written book by Mark

Wolynn. In this book, he reveals story after story of his own traumas shaped by the Armenian genocide. The roots of these difficulties did not reside in his own experience but in the lives of his parents and grandparents.

I now understand why, for most of my life, I have felt completely out of alignment. I felt as if I lived in someone else's skin, like something was blocked. Something felt resistant inside my body, but I never knew what this was. I ignored it. I pushed it away. I bought just one more new thing that was either put in my closet with the tags still on or I gave it away barely used. Credit cards became maxed out, I exercised until my body broke down, and I sought validation in many areas of my life. I didn't want to feel what was within me. I didn't even want to admit I had any issues. I knew nothing back then that would have given me a clue of this inherited energy that didn't belong to me. Yet, I felt an uncomfortable sensation of fear in my body, a fear of failure that crippled me from achieving my life goals.

When was the last time the messages from the world talked about healing from the inside first? When we are born, we are perfect beings. Seeing ourselves as these perfect beings isn't the clear message we are taught. When was the last time we were measured for who we are, not what we can accomplish or what we look like? We are not taught this. We are not taught that failure is part of success. Perfectionism is the only reality. In my childhood I was so afraid to fail that I didn't want to try anything new. In my adult life I became a "dabbler." I dabbled in my small businesses, in my schooling, or creative adventures, but never completed anything in fear that if I tried, I would fail, and if I failed, I would not be loved. Therefore, I lived in this feeling of frustration and empty dreams.

I can remember my mother had that same characteristic as her father, especially toward me—the characteristic of living through the accomplishments of their children. Of course, we all have a different interpretation of how we react to someone else. We can be raised by the same parent but have a completely different outcome.

Her father was not able to show his affection nor accept any of my mother's dreams. Her mother's voice was not heard. She was sweet, quiet, and unassuming, so my mother inherited the characteristics of her father. The dreams of pursuing her passion for horses was discouraged. She had a belief that her father didn't approve of her life no matter what she did. Her eldest brother was thought of as the success in the family, pursuing a career in the English Army. My brave mother exported herself from the comforts and familiarity of home to travel from England to Bermuda, to live with a family and take care of the children as their nanny. She was helped by a friend who ended up becoming her most trusted confidant throughout her life. Making her way to a place unknown and becoming a nanny was not her dream, but it was a way to physically escape the disapproved life she was living. Her need to see her children flourish where she did not was part of her pain throughout her life.

Experiencing her children's "failure" was a direct reflection of herself. As an adult, I understand all she tried to do. Though my mom died in England twenty-one years ago, I can still remember her sweet words to me before she passed: "I was a good mother, wasn't I?" With tears welling up in my eyes as I held her hand one last time, I reassured her that she was. Her greatest achievement was to love the three of her children in a way that seemed foreign. She tried the best way she could. All parents do. She died with a feeling of accomplishment in her English cottage, in a small village with winding roads and a small post office where she could buy milk and cheese for breakfast.

Not healing from those old, limited stories that make us feel less than or not good enough will keep us imprisoned in an unfulfilled life. We can only make these changes and shifts when we awaken to new possibilities. When we begin believing there are new possibilities that will move us to the truth of who we are, we live in absolute freedom to be the human we were birthed to be.

In the pursuit of your own healing, *At a Glance* below will help unearth where you might be feeling stuck. Further on, I will explain in depth about our seven energy centers or chakras.

If you wish to understand yourself deeper, I have provided an *energetic assessment quiz* for you to understand where you may be blocked and what needs to be healed within you. This could be the reason you may not be feeling fulfilled in your life, be feeling overwhelmed and stressed, have low energy, or just not feel like yourself. Just scan your phone over the code and follow the prompts.

At a Glance

- If you are experiencing a feeling of insecurity about finances or your basic needs and well-being, your root chakra may be blocked.
- If you are experiencing a lack of creative inspiration and life feels dull, your sacral chakra may be blocked.
- If you are experiencing low self-esteem and not feeling good enough, your solar plexus chakra may be blocked.
- If you are experiencing trust issues or you are holding on to grudges, your heart chakra may be blocked.
- If you are experiencing difficulty expressing your thoughts, your throat chakra may be blocked.
- If you are experiencing yourself slipping into judgmental thoughts frequently, your third eye chakra may be blocked.
- If you are experiencing trouble trusting the universe or believing in a higher power, your crown chakra may be blocked.

Chapter 3

The Art of Meditation

The First Step to Healing

The connection to our quiet center is where healing can begin. The daily practice of meditation allows us to arrive at this inner center of ourselves with more clarity, peace, and focus. It can help us slow down, take in what is going on around us, and really learn to appreciate our lives. Meditation is also a tool that can help us change for the better—whether we are looking to destress, give up bad habits, or find new perspectives.

Becoming aware of our thoughts is how we understand what we are mentally attaching to and in what we are believing. It is understandable this process can be challenging to the beginning meditator. On average, we think over 70,000 thoughts every day, so it's no wonder we can't concentrate. It's no wonder we feel tangled in the vines in our heads. Without quiet examination, these thoughts can feel as if we are somehow caught in a snow globe and we can't see our way out. The only thing we experience is the emotion. Our thoughts create what we are reacting to. Meditation allows us to see and listen.

How it Helped Me

For too many years I was controlled by thoughts that held me back from reaching my goals and loving myself deeply. These thoughts led me to believe I wasn't beautiful, that I couldn't be anything I put my mind to. I was asleep to the fact that my inner language was like cement that camouflaged my inner golden light. The practice of meditation allowed me to calm my mind and to take a step back from my thoughts and be a witness to my inner narrative.

When most of us think of meditation, we may think it's about deep chanting that lasts for hours. We may see images of monks cloaked in red frocks, silent for hours, or imagine sitting in a very uncomfortable cross-legged position until our legs have no feeling. Meditation has gotten a bad rap.

When someone first suggested I would benefit from meditation, I began making all the excuses as to why I couldn't begin. I didn't have time. I didn't know how. I thought it meant I had to take a vow of poverty, eat roots from the earth, or leave my armpits unshaven. These were all myths that stopped me not only from changing my life, but from *saving* my life.

Meditation saved me from living life believing in thoughts that were not true, disconnected from the truth of who I was. My mind was filled with so many thoughts I wasn't sure how to begin. With the help of my meditation teacher, I began the step-by-step process of finding silence and stillness. My teacher showed up in my life because I was ready. He was a very well-established meditation guide who has helped thousands of people find their quiet center.

Opening myself up to the possibility of making meditation my new daily practice took time. With consistency and having a spiritual teacher to hold me accountable, I began each morning with a ritual of the practice. I started first with five minutes, and eventually built my practice to sitting for one hour every day. Just sitting and noticing the thoughts that would swirl in my head was the start, then being completely present to the inhale and exhale of my breath. The beautiful experience of meditation is personal, and we each get to make it our own. There is neither a right nor wrong way when we are building this daily habit.

The richness and abundance that meditation brings to our lives is intangible. It is a feeling, one we cannot purchase or hang on a wall for others to admire. The feeling is priceless, and it will allow us to energetically vibrate from an entirely new place.

I want to offer you one of my favorite ways to begin meditating. Try this:

Sit comfortably in an upright position. Gently close your eyes and take a deep inhale, and then an exhale. Bring your awareness to the sounds around you and focus on the variety of noises near and far from you. If thoughts begin to show up, just bring your attention to a bird singing, or a car engine, or maybe the wind blowing in the trees. Start off with five minutes and work your way to as long as you can go without feeling overwhelmed.

How to Get Started

Intention Setting

To arrive at this place of inner stillness and truth, we begin by setting an intention. We hear that word repeated over and over, but do we actually know what it is? I define an intention as a determination or plan to do something specific. There is a difference between an intention and a goal. The goal is what you concretely achieve, whereas an intent is the process you go through or a willful direction. What is your specific intent? To feel calmer? To understand your thoughts or to wear cute yoga pants you bought in your favorite store? Your intent for beginning a practice gets to be your own.

When I began meditating daily, I wanted to understand why I felt so out of balance in my emotions and in my physical body and why I was reacting defensively to my then husband and why I felt so much anger. This feeling I began noticing was not in alignment with me, and I wanted to understand what these thoughts were that birthed the emotions that kept me in a cage of confinement.

Whatever your reason for beginning, it is perfect.

Once I understood that my intent was to feel calmer and understand my thoughts, I wrote down ways I knew would get me there. When we see our words in front of us, they become even more powerful. Meditation was what I chose. Finding all the resources that would facilitate the beginning process helped me to stay on track. The powerful art of journaling takes the attachment away from the words. When you write it down, you can begin understanding what you're reacting to.

Baby Steps

In my coaching, I hear my clients wanting to take giant leaps in their healing. They ask, "How long will this take?" The need to want to heal faster or to take huge steps forward is normal but understand that big leaps can crash-land you into overwhelm. When we begin any type of new habit, we take our time and make small, powerful steps to our destination. Our culture dictates that the fastest and biggest is the only way to experience life. I can remember this happening to me when I considered quieting my mind ten years ago.

When I began my practice, I didn't know about moderation or those small steps I just shared with you. Like everything I do, I give 120 percent of my effort into the task at hand. I can remember setting that intention that was way too much when beginning my peace journey. I told myself that I needed to meditate for the first time for exactly an hour. I had seen countless suggestions in magazines I kept next to my bed. Anything less than an hour was not good enough. I would feel like a failure if I didn't succeed in what I set out to do.

I sat down on my wooden meditation chair with the engraved Sanskrit down the arm. I had purchased this exquisite chair from one of those expensive wellness catalogs that get jammed in your mailbox. My new yoga pants with the Buddha painted on each leg were a perfect fit and made me look like I knew what I was doing. I always thought that one must look the part. I lit my special peace candle and burned an incense that had been in my bedside table since my last attempt at being a meditation guru. With the most recent copy of *Meditation Today* magazine next to me, just in case I had to refer to the section on starting a practice, I sat for the longest minute of my life.

The guided visualization I began listening to only opened the floodgate doors of thought. My head was instantly flooded by one thought and then another and another. I was overwhelmed. I vowed that I couldn't experience this peace everyone was always talking about, and I convinced myself that I would be the only one in the world who wouldn't be able to experience peace. I would have to live forever with this unsettled mind and never be able to enjoy my so-called life. Ugh!

This, of course, turned out to be a lie.

Think of a staircase. When you are climbing stairs, you don't leap to the top. You take each stair first until you reach the top. This is your first step.

This Is What I Did

Make a grid on a piece of paper or on your phone calendar. Set aside five minutes every day for a week to sit, to pause, to do nothing except breathe. Allow yourself to sit in the same spot at the same time each morning. When that five minutes feels comfortable, add another five minutes to your time for the next week. Stick with the time. Your ego will want you to do more only to overwhelm you, so you stop. Keep adding each week until you are meditating and not even thinking about it.

Your ego is afraid of you quieting down. The true light of who you are is behind those old stories that keep you in their grip.

Pick Your Sacred Space

This step is my favorite. Creating a sacred space that invites more peace and calm in your life will change the chemistry in your body. The space we share with our outer environment reflects what we feel on the inside. One is connected to the other.

I can remember before I began my spiritual awakening, my outer environment reflected a very confused and disorganized young mother. The walls of my home then do not reflect my environment now. My mind was cluttered with thoughts. My outer environment was cluttered with stuff; from the clutter jammed into drawers and closets, to the endless racks of clothes just purchased from my favorite store.

In the process of healing, we not only get to "clear" the headspace on the inside, but we get to "clear" our sacred spaces on the outside. When we are beginning to practice the art of meditation, we want to sit in a place that evokes the emotions we wish to feel. Choosing to meditate in a place of quiet and calm, rather than in a place with clutter and disorganization, will allow us to make the transition to peace easier and with more flow.

Match how you are feeling to the world in which you live.

This Is What I Did

There were so many places in my home that could have been perfect to create my meditation space. I was fortunate to have a large house that offered me seclusion—seclusion from the voices of my children asking when dinner was going to be ready, seclusion from the dogs wandering around my house wondering where I had disappeared to. Any spot you choose is perfect. Just make sure you aren't disturbed. Let your family know that only if the house is burning down or if someone is choking, are you to be disturbed.

Designate the same spot every morning to be where you land. Surround yourself with things that bring you joy. In my space I surrounded myself with Buddhas that I had collected all around the world. Whatever you choose is perfect. Maybe you choose your space outside under an old oak tree in your front yard or on your porch with those old rocking chairs your grandmother gave you or in your bathroom that has that deadbolt you had newly installed. Wherever the space, it's perfect. Just pick that sacred space.

Choose Your Type

Look in any wellness magazine or listen to any meditation podcast and you will discover the many different types of meditation. There are meditations for anxiety, meditations for self-worth, or even meditation for when your in-laws come into town, and you need a quick dose of escapism. It can completely confuse the average person trying to begin a practice. How do you find the right type for you?

When I began searching for how I wanted to experience my quiet center, I began with an app that allowed me to search for many different kinds, with many different voices. I tried Zen meditation, the type that encourages complete silence. I tried guided, where you listen to someone's voice take you to a place of inner stillness. I tried mantra meditation, where you say a positive affirmation over and over again. I have tried them all and have decided after many years that sitting in silence is the best type for me. I sit for sometimes ten minutes and sometimes for hours, welcoming any passing thoughts to enter my mind space. There is a myth out there that insists when in meditation, we cannot have *any* thoughts. That is impossible! The way I have trained myself is to think of a wave. When I notice the thought wave coming in, I focus on my breath and think of the wave going out. This helps me to not become attached to the thought and therefore create an emotion that would take me down that road of endless stories. Becoming the "watcher" of thought helps you to not become the thought. It is truly a blessing to be able to experience this.

Be the blue sky. Your thoughts are the clouds. Like a soft breeze, gently exhale your clouds of thoughts.

I opened to the possibility of trying as many versions of meditation that I could. I was determined to do it my way and not be persuaded to like a specific type just because one style was trendier than the next. Listen to yourself and learn to honor what your voice is telling you.

The Afterthought of My Practice

When I think of who I am now after creating my daily practice, the story of the Golden Buddha comes to mind. The story is about uncovering the light or solid gold that we all are. This is the me that I have stepped into.

I am going to share with you the version that I have understood. It is a true story.

In 1957, an entire monastery was moved by a group of monks. One day they were moving a giant clay Buddha when one of the monks noticed a large crack in the clay. Upon closer examination he noticed golden light emanating from the old cracking cement. The old cracking cement began falling away with the slightest touch. The monk began using a hammer and chisel to chip away the false layer to reveal that the statue was solid gold.

The Golden Buddha had been covered with cement by the Thai monks to protect it from the invading Burmese army. The monks had all been killed but the great Buddha had survived.

When we learn how to quiet our minds in meditation, we are able to understand the cement that covers our golden light. The cement represents the limiting stories we believe from someone else's pain, the pain from our family of origin that hasn't been chiseled away.

I have become the light that I knew was from my earliest memory as a child. I was able to be present to my thoughts, understand which thoughts were my own, and which thoughts didn't belong to me so I could change my emotions. I feel joy. I feel happiness, and I feel as if I can take on the world shining my light from within.

Every single one of us has that light underneath the layers and layers of clay. We all have those hammers and chisels that can chip away the old conditioning from parents, teachers, and society that will reveal our highest potential. It is our choice to believe this is a possibility to start uncovering the layers.

Meditation was the uncovering for me. It didn't just change my life, but it saved my life.

Chapter 4

The Mystic Healer

Expanding into myself, I opened a door to understanding the energy inside my body. That energy with which I was identified from childhood was now ready to be revealed. I understood on a small scale about my inner energy from my training as a Reiki healer. I was now eager to study my practice in a deeper and more reflective way. If you are not familiar with Reiki or energy healing, it is a Japanese technique that promotes healing through the hands of practitioners, to promote energetic balance physically, emotionally, mentally, and spiritually. The practice promotes relaxation and helps release the grip of energy in the seven centers of our bodies, improving overall health and well-being.

I will explain about our energy centers in more detail further in this chapter, so stay tuned. I felt in my soul that I wanted to uplevel my ability to offer this hands-on healing to my clients as well as myself. I was fascinated when I began studying with an online school, about the energies we hold in our bodies. The idea that we can heal ourselves by releasing old stagnation created by traumas we experience in childhood fascinated me. After completing my practical studies, I decided two years later that I wanted to have a deeper hands-on training. Hence, my greatest lesson.

This Is What I Did

It was the beginning of March 2020. You know, the year that never really existed. There was a collective sigh that COVID would never affect us here in the states. Boy were we wrong!

I packed my bag for a short trip, knowing I wouldn't need much for an uneventful week of meditative silence. I had registered for a silent meditation retreat deep in the woods of southern California near Big Sur. Flying from one side of the country to California, I attended the retreat, with great enthusiasm, following all the prompts to stay silent during my stay there.

The last night of my visit I went out to dinner with some friends in town visiting me. There, sitting quietly in the corner was a man who definitely did not look like he belonged in this trendy restaurant with tiny glass chandeliers hanging over each cozy table. He caught my eye, and I was intrigued by his stature and how he presented himself. His hair was pulled up into a ponytail that sat on top of his head. Beaded bracelets adorned his wrists. Mala necklaces hung down his sturdy chest. My friends and I sat behind him at a small table with a freshly cut flower arrangement and a candle that danced and flickered from the fan above. As I sat there listening to my friends talk about their harrowing drive north, I could feel some sort of energy around me that I couldn't explain. It was a force somehow flowing from this stranger sitting by himself, to the inner core of my soul.

When we finished our meal, there was something drawing me closer to him. I could feel something churning within that I needed to find out who this man was and why I felt this energetic charge toward him. It was not because I had just shifted out of a thirty-year marriage, and I was eager to start dating. That was the farthest thing from my mind. Some of you may be rolling your eyes at this, but my intent was all about spiritual healing, and I felt this man was there to show me my new light.

I asked the restaurant owner who the man was sitting alone at a table by himself. He was writing in a leather journal embellished with sacred stones that glimmered in the candlelight. The owner was generous with details about this stranger that created my mental buzz. The stranger in the corner was one of the most renowned mystic healers in the area. He ran a healing school nearby along the sweeping coastline of Big Sur. This healer was there at a perfect time to show me more about myself. I firmly believe that "the teacher appears when the student is ready." I was ready. There are some people who show up in our lives that we cherish and grow with for the majority of our lives. Others become what I call our "lesson friends," who show up for a brief time, so we can learn more about ourselves. He was one of those lesson friends.

As I began to walk out of the restaurant, I made the bold move to his table. He reeked of sage and sandalwood as he turned toward me to stare directly into my eyes. The presence of his energy was nothing like I had ever experienced. The encounter with this man was so unfamiliar that it made me want to run away, drive to the airport, and return home to safety. I didn't, because I was listening to the voice within gently encouraging me forward to experience something that would change the trajectory of my life. That gentle yet invisible voice was driving me to explore the depths of myself through the energy healing of Reiki, and this mystic healer showed up at the perfect time. The pulse of curiosity was at its peak.

I asked for his information so I could contact him and perhaps begin learning from this master healer. He reached for a paper napkin and wrote with a borrowed pen from the bar. His handwriting was difficult to read. I squinted to see his name, Josef Crown. He also shared his landline phone number that seemed to date back to 1982. He had no website to share nor any fancy social media hashtags. We spoke briefly, and he was happy to offer me a space to come study with him.

The country began to shut down, and I didn't want to travel back to the East Coast. There was no one at home waiting for me or anyone expecting me to return at any given time. I had begun to explore myself without the confines of a marriage. I could make decisions without affecting anyone else. I was free, yet I was entering a very frightening time of the unknown—not just with COVID that had begun to seep into the country and lockdowns beginning to become a part of our daily lives, but also I was beginning to transform myself without the safety of my normal life. I felt as if I were free falling and had no idea if there would be anything or anyone to hold the net for me before I hit the ground. I had to believe I would be safe.

There were the skeptics who shared their opinions and advised me strongly not to take this inspired action and come home immediately. I was even told by my well-meaning sister that I had joined a religious cult and Josef was holding me against my will. Instead, I listened to my inner voice and headed the next evening to the dwelling of this mystic stranger.

After a sleepless night and a day of reorganizing travel plans, I gathered the belongings I had packed for the week-long retreat and headed that evening to my new residence at the home of this strange healer. We made arrangements for me to stay at his personal residence in the middle of the redwoods in the seclusion of nature. I began my drive to his home, winding around the treacherous roads along Highway 1 that would have put me off even in the daylight. The night was so dark along the route, and it was hard to navigate on my GPS (Global Positioning System). There were no lights anywhere along the stretch of road leading south. The only lighter part of the darkness was the sky in the far distance over the ocean. The cliffs below awaited unexpected drivers who might become distracted.

My GPS signaled me to turn off of the main highway. Turning my newly rented car to the left, I took a little inhale and fear crept into my gut. The narrow road to his house seemed so unfamiliar and secluded. I wanted to turn back. *What was I thinking? This is crazy. Everyone who warned me was right.*

My GPS confirmed I would arrive just around the next corner. My mystic healer told me to look for two red lion heads at the end of the driveway. As I made that final turn around the dark and unknown corner, the red majestic lion heads stood at the end of the driveway, as promised. As I pulled into the driveway, careful not to hit the rails of the little bridge stretching across the babbling stream, I looked up, and sitting in the woods was a modest house perched on top of a bank. The lights were on outside. The walkway to this humble dwelling was lit with red, orange, yellow, green, blue, indigo and white lights. All the colors of the seven chakra energy centers in the body were illuminated. My personal illumination and discovery was about to be unearthed and healed for good.

Upon arrival, I remember uttering some fearful words to him, as I felt completely intimidated as he walked to my car to greet me. In a sheepish voice, I said, "This is so weird! I do not feel comfortable. You could be a serial killer." I felt so much fear I don't even remember how he responded.

Josef then led me to my sacred space in which I would spend the next three months. The space was comfortable but void of any extravagance. There was a pull-out couch, a tiny kitchenette, and a toilet and shower. The artwork consisted of the redwoods outside, that danced together in swaying unison. Nature was full of life just outside of the large glass windows. It was as if I were one with the only company that would visit me throughout my stay at this stranger's residence.

Each morning we agreed to begin our studies at 8 a.m. sharp. I was strongly reminded that I was never to arrive a minute too early or a minute too late. There was a curated breakfast, a prayer to the Divine before we began eating, and then the study would begin at exactly 9 a.m. I felt so awkward as we sat in silence for most of the meals. Sometimes he would ask a very complicated question that I had to answer with my limited understanding.

Each morning he would be dressed in crisp white linen with a fantastically colorful scarf wrapped around his neck. Those same mala necklaces I had seen on the first encounter still hung from his strong, thick neck. He was never clean-shaven, and body deodorant was not abundantly used.

The inside of his home was heated by his small fireplace that he would meticulously stoke with a long metal pole. His house was dark and filled with treasures that hung from the walls and organically placed on bookshelves that wrapped around the small living room.

With endless days of tears, I began to understand my deeply rooted stories I had been identifying with and where in my body I was unknowingly storing the energetic debris of old limitations and worry that kept me stuck. Remember, I didn't think I could accomplish anything. I was always afraid of failing. I was not good enough. Those were the stories I learned to clear and not believe in. I healed my fear story that I thought was a part of me.

One day, I was sent out into the woods alone, crossing a rain-filled river with bare feet and carrying my heavy backpack filled with various stones and wood to perform a "remote" Reiki session with someone who lived in Germany. This is a practice of energy healing that can be experienced with a healer and a client from afar. I had arranged with Ingrid that we would meet at the same time and begin the practice of Reiki as if she were lying in front of me. I can remember trying to think of any excuse I could so I didn't have to experience this and feel uncomfortable. My healer didn't want to hear it. I felt the fear and did it anyway.

Off I went to this abandoned beach that I had to walk three miles to get to in the rain with bare feet. I created my *energy grid* out of stones and sticks I collected from the beach. At the agreed time of 10 a.m., I sat in meditation energetically connecting to the woman from Germany. The rain soaked my entire body as I sat silently connecting to each energy center I had created in the sand. After the thirty-minute session in my mind with the stranger I only knew from a telephone conversation, I began to feel relaxed, grounded, and in complete energetic flow.

With my rain-soaked clothes and hair matted to my head, I gathered my heavy backpack and made the long hike back to my car. Through the swelled stream, down the stony pathway, and through all the muddy puddles in bare feet, there in the distance was my red rental car. The moment I saw it sitting alone in the parking lot, I felt a surge of completion. An old cord was somehow severed by my discomfort. I did it. I didn't allow the energy of fear to stop me. Warming my frozen feet with the heater was my greatest reward, and at that moment my relationship with fear had shifted.

With the wisdom and guidance of my healer, I began to understand the connection between my trauma stories and my energy chakra centers. My body seemed to be calling out to me to start listening. I had some chronic health conditions that kept emerging, and I knew I could heal myself through inner awareness. I am not a doctor, but I am one who, through the years, has healed many physical issues that dominated my life. All because I journeyed deeper into the woman waiting to be released from what didn't belong to her. Energy is a part of each and every one of us. The energy we live with can belong to and vibrate from our esoteric self or we can continue to live a life connected to unhealed energy from someone else.

The Magic of Energy Healing

Before I began this inner journey in Big Sur, I had no idea about the energetics we all hold in our bodies. What were they talking about when they used the word "chakra"? This foreign word sounded like a Spanish translation for some sort of dance style that beautiful women, dressed in red ruffled skirts, would offer to their uncommitted lovers. That, of course, was not quite right.

Our energy centers, or chakras, in our bodies are one of the most important areas to heal ourselves. The example that comes to my mind when I explain healed energy is that our body is like a river. The seven chakras that play the greatest role are positioned in the center of our bodies. The main chakra system consists of seven energy wheels that spin and spread energy in the environment that surrounds the body. These wheels also take energy from the outside world and distribute it to the blood, the main glands, the organs, and the nervous centers. If the specific energy center is blocked, we may experience " dis-ease" or feel completely uncomfortable in our own skin. We do have many meridians and chakras connected to our physical body, but this book would turn into a scientific dissertation if I explained them all. They are centered in a straight line from the top of your head through the base of your lower foundation. Each one holds on to and is in charge of many different emotional energies.

*Key below reads from bottom to top

🔵 Root Chakra: Security, Survival

🔵 Sacral Chakra: Sensuality, Creativity

🔵 Solar Plexus Chakra: Confidence, Personal Power

🔵 Heart Chakra: Compassion, Love

🔵 Throat Chakra: Truth, Communication

🔵 Third Eye Chakra: Insight, Intuition

🔵 Crown Chakra: Enlightenment, Spirituality

The healthy way chakras work is to gently receive and release energies from experiences we encounter from childhood into the lives we live now. Most of our trauma is experienced when we are children. The pain and trauma energy from childhood is then carried into our life as adults.

After my experience in Big Sur I started to take a deeper look into my energy chakra centers. My body seemed to be calling out to me to start listening to chronic health conditions that kept emerging. Again, I am not a doctor, but I am one who believes trauma and pain can cause disease in our bodies. I can happily say that I have now healed myself by clearing the reservoir that was jammed with all the debris of the past.

The Basic Principles of the Chakra System

The Root Chakra

This energy center is related to survival and security, and is the closest to the earth, resting at the base of the spine. This center is where we hold on to the energetic pain and trauma we experience as children. The color associated with it is red. It is naturally associated with the element earth. To keep this chakra healthy and in flow, exercises such as dancing, jogging, or jumping are beneficial. We should see if our security needs are being met and take our power to create our own security in our lives so our world is a safe and enjoyable place for us. Its message is, "I exist." Live your life proudly.

The Sacral Chakra

This chakra is related to sensuality, sexuality, and desire for pleasure. It is in the lower abdomen and its color is orange and is associated with the element water. Belly dancing, loving partnerships, and yoga can enhance this chakra's function. This chakra says, "I desire." Live your passion, whatever that may be. What are your dreams? How do you desire to live? Claim your dreams and go out and make them a reality—give birth to your dreams.

The Solar Plexus

Its color is yellow, and it is related to our power in this world. Its natural element is fire, and this is where the "fire in your belly" term derives from. An overbearing solar plexus chakra (one not in balance with your system's other chakras or one where your energy is solely focused) can result in obsessive-compulsive control. A solar plexus chakra with a healthy flow allows you to control your destiny, feel your power, and accomplish your dreams. The message of the third chakra is, "I control." Go forth and control your own destiny and happiness—you deserve it!

The Heart Chakra

Green is the color of this chakra, and it relates naturally to love and compassion, being at our heart's center. This fourth chakra is associated with air. Healthy relationships, pets, family, and even appreciation of beauty and nature enhance the health of this chakra. Let your heart energy flow freely in and out. Be open to receiving the love available to you now, the free-flowing love that is your birthright. Sense your Reiki family around the world—feel the great love you all share and selflessly emanate into this world. Shine the love that you are. Repeat, "I am love."

The Throat Chakra

The throat center or communication center is where you speak your truth in this world. Its color is blue. When this chakra flows at optimum levels, you have the ability to ask for what you need. This chakra also reflects your truth in the world through your communication. Singing, chanting, and breathing exercises can enhance this chakra's health. The message of the throat chakra is, "I express." Do not suppress your own beautiful voice. Speak your truth, sing your joy, and emanate your love through the vibration of your words.

The Third Eye

The natural color of this chakra is indigo. Insight, intuition, awareness, and guidance are the properties of this sixth chakra. Located between the eyebrows, this chakra says, "I am the witness." Meditation and visualization exercises can assist the healthy flow of this chakra. Be open to your inner guidance. Listen to your thoughts. They will assist you on the right path.

The Crown Chakra

It is the silence between the spaces and represents spiritual connection. It is associated with violet or violet-white light, a color many Reiki practitioners are drawn to and use in their work and meditations. Located a little above the top of the head, it represents union, bliss, and the knowledge of being at one with all. Cosmic consciousness and peace are the frequencies at this chakra, which says, "I am that I am."

This Is What I Did

When we are new at healing, we may not understand that energy can be healed by being present to the sensation we feel in our bodies. A new meditation practice allows us to get quiet and be present to the charge or the sensation that bubbles up. Every story we tell ourselves has a charge to it that will show up in a certain place in our bodies.

The "I'm not enough" story might show up in your stomach area, your solar plexus or personal power center. The sensation might feel like a nauseous stomach that you quickly remedy with some quick-fix meditation. Go deeper. Understand that your body gives you signs at any given moment. Start to listen, and you will live a life of ease, calm, and flow.

Here is a quick little meditation reminder:

Breathing healing energy into your chakras, starting at the base, seeing the colors vividly, and visualizing your beautiful energy centers absorbing the color like a sponge, fill your body with health, wisdom, and light. Beginning at the red root chakra and then rising with each color all the way up to your crown, breathe in the colors of each center. As you rise to each area, remember to place your own healing hands at each point, feeling the warmth from your hands. Fill yourself with peace, calm, and forgiveness. You can say to yourself when you place your hands gently on each point, "I am okay. I am safe. I am loved."

On the other side of healing, my stories of internal energy have allowed me to feel calm, peaceful, happy, full of joy, and full of love. I have ascended to the highest version of myself. So can you!

Chapter 5

Your Inner Story—Healing and Reparenting

In our journey to truth, we are all privileged to have another chance to feel better about ourselves—to feel more grounded, deeper love, and that sense of empowerment. No, we cannot change the way we were raised, but we can change how we treat that little one inside of all of us now. This is the art of *reparenting,* where we allow ourselves to be parented by our adult selves the way our inner child longed to be raised, and that would have catapulted us into greatness.

Can you imagine yourself without that limited voice that doubts every move you make? Can you imagine what you would have accomplished and what dreams you could have made come true if you believed in your inner voice at an early age? Yes, we can feel successful in our career or in relationships.

Are we experiencing our lives with our own truths or the truths of someone else? Imagine a world where we all have our own purpose without any shoulds, coulds, or maybes. Reparenting has helped the little girl in me come out from the inner darkness and into her magical star magnificence. Her inner light was dimmed to the point that there was no spark anymore. That deep, dark basement she was hiding in was a place of safe refuge for the majority of her life. Even though the basement was in her own mind, she had forgotten how to ignite that inner light until the voice was completely altered.

Remembering Your Light

I want to introduce you to this sweet little girl again. Remember that little sweet girl in the gingham shirt with a short pixie haircut, the sticks-and-leaves-in-her-hair kind of girl. Yes, my identity was molded from my riding experience I wrote about in chapter one. But, as an adult, I get to experience a "do-over" and parent my inner child the way I had wished I had been parented. We all have that ability, but first we get to understand our own inner story. I sought validation from the outside in order to feel what I longed for on the inside. The only way we can do that is to create the experience ourselves, not waiting for others to create it for us. Take the time and begin listening. Hear that voice screaming for you to be kind. Be loving. Be inspirational.

That Inner Language

Do you ever notice how you speak to yourself? That invisible person inside your head that dictates the language we identify with can be so familiar, especially when it's not nice. That language can be carried from our childhood, and we then parent our inner selves with exactly the same vocabulary we grew up with. Words are powerful and can imprison us in a space of limitations, not being enough, and self-hatred.

Our inner dialogue can be birthed by childhood memories. Virgin ears hear and then create the dialogue we grow up listening to. The language we identify with is commonly created by the inner language of those people who influence our lives; family or peers are usually the most dedicated teachers.

My dear mother was not the only person in my life who mirrored the identity that would be a part of my soul. My siblings, as well as my juvenile peers, set the course of how I began speaking to myself. These misinterpretations held me back from being the person I so longed to believe in. Instead, the empty echoes of negativity were what I related myself to.

I can remember one of the many identities that shaped my young mind came from riding the bus. My bus ride to and from school did not fill me with joyful memories. It was a time when bullying was not taken as seriously as it is taken today. As I climbed onto the bus, with my little red shoes and sparkly backpack, I sat in the front seat near the friendly bus driver with the hairnet gently tucked under her hat. The upright seat and her friendly smile became my safe refuge from the daily chanting.

Instead of positive chants of maybe "Sarah Sunshine" or Sarah Sparkle," I witnessed negative teasing. "Sarah Sewer," as in toilet, was my designated name. My peers who tended to sit in the back space of the bus, made sure everyone was in sync, chanting as I climbed fearfully onto the bus.

As an adult, I understand these names are nothing but a reflection of pain and hurt in the dozens of these chanting children. They didn't seem to care when they saw this little girl shed a tear down her face. This was an everyday occurrence for this little eight-year-old full of inner sparkle and joy. I even tried to miss the bus each morning, pretending to forget my lunch box my mother had carefully packed for me. The sandwich and fruit were packed into an old, plastic bread bag. My mother still lived in the era of reusing "perfectly usable containers." Oh, how I wished my mom would use those cool zip lock bags I saw other children using at the lunch table. I was already marked as "Sarah Sewer," and now this!

The negative words from my bus escapades continued until I graduated from my beloved school, East Bradford. The stories I was believing in from elementary school followed me into middle school and high school. The experiences of talking to boys, getting good grades, and being popular were different from my earlier youth, but the feelings I was having about myself were the same. I was not good at any of those three things, as I explored a new and mature version of myself. I was shy with boys to the point that speaking to them would break me out in a cold sweat. I was very quiet and only hung out with my very best friend, Emily, and maybe one or two other friends who were as awkward as me. The good grades part of high school was shaped by another voice I began to listen to, my brother who was a math whiz. I was not. His constant teasing that I was "stupid" was another imposter I allowed to visit the room in my head.

At such a tender age, I didn't know how to defend myself from the name calling, the names that became me. Instead, I began believing I was stupid, and that title followed me and haunted me even into my college years. I never finished college because of the fear that I would fail, have to take math, and be shamed by someone else who could also call me stupid.

Words are powerful. When we are young, we don't understand how powerful they can be. As adults we can recognize the power of these limiting words and become aware of how the old stories can hold us back. With this awareness, we can take an inventory of how our voices make us feel. We can "reparent" those old voices that scream negativity from within and use language to lift us up and inspire us to feel good about ourselves.

This Is What I Did

I began being present to the sensation I was feeling in my body. You know, that feeling when we say, "I just don't feel like *myself.*" Sometimes it was triggered by what someone said to me. Sometimes I would feel the charge when I believed in that negative voice in my head—the voice that had prevented me from reaching the stars and believing that everything I dreamed of was possible.

When you feel that misaligned sensation, take a breath and become aware of what you are thinking. Remember, what you think creates the charge or heaviness in your body. Right at that moment is when you can "reparent" or change your inner vocabulary and create a more positive and upbeat emotion. So when you notice yourself saying, "You're stupid," "You're ugly," or whatever that old language included, you can become the parent you have longed for and instead say, "You're brilliant," "You're beautiful," or "You're enough." Noticing the language and mindfully saying the opposite is a very effective practice. Try it. The experience will change your life. After all the meditation you must be adding to your life, you are now quiet enough to take that emotional step back and listen. Your little self will thank you!

The Inner Child Meditation

*Gently close your eyes and begin bringing your awareness to
your breath. Simply breathe in peaceful, calm energy and
exhale anything creating resistance that wants to go. Drop your
focus to the space around your heart. Understand that in this
space is your true self, your authenticity. Your heart is now full
of love. You might even want to visualize a color in that area.*

*Just breathe here and relax . . . picture that little you, the
earliest memory that comes to mind. See her/him before you.
What is she/he wearing? How old is this little you? Let this
little being stand in front of you and see her/him in your
mind's eye. Visualize your adult self standing next to this
younger version of you. Maybe you are sitting on a park bench
surrounded by beautiful flowers with bees buzzing hungrily
to each flower. Maybe you see your adult self walking hand
in hand with your sweet inner child in a beautiful, wooded
haven. Wherever you are, allow your inner self to feel safe here
with you. You might even sense her/him relaxing and taking
deep, calming breaths. Feel that peace and calm in both of
you. You might even turn, smile, and squeeze her/his hand and
notice that you both have become one.*

Taking Care of Self

Another important part of reparenting and healing is how well we
take care of our physical and mental needs. The way we "treat" ourselves
as adults reflects how we treated ourselves growing up.

Who served as your role model? Who was your reflection of self-care?

I know that I modeled my dear mom's way of caring for herself. There
was no fun, no resting, and no taking naps. She was identified with her

doing. How much she accomplished was how she felt about her inner value. Self-care was not something she valued. She had to be busy even when her life began to crumble.

When my father left our family to pursue another life on his own, I remember my mother sitting on the floor in our cold living room, cleaning her saddles, while tears flowed down her cheeks. There was no time even in her sadness to take care of herself and maybe wrap herself in a soft blanket, drink a soothing cup of tea, or take a hot bubble bath to soothe the pain away. The antidote was to force herself to work harder and resist any type of loving self-care. I modeled this behavior.

Over time, I realized the importance of slowing ourselves down and allowing that inner self time to relax and recharge. That little self has been carrying the load for you all your life and is now ready for you to take care of her or him. Your adult self is in charge now. She/he can allow your inner child to take a break. Take an inner vacation and feel the difference.

The idea of putting our needs before others' and giving our souls oxygen first is foreign for so many of us. Not caring for ourselves has become an epidemic. We are left witnessing a stressed-out, depleted society so tired that we convince ourselves we don't even have time to take care of that exhausted, inner child. Our bodies are breaking down. We react and attach to negative emotions. We fill our bodies with junk food and expect ourselves to live abundant lives. It's time to pause and take inventory of how we treat ourselves.

This Is What I Did

Write a list of ways to care for yourself, specifically ways you and your inner self will feel taken care of. Self-care does not have to be a huge leap or cost a lot of money. Sometimes the smallest thing like having a cup of tea in a quiet environment, wrapping yourself in a cozy blanket, or taking yourself out for a delicious lunch can be all your self needs. This care can be slowing down and living life with mindfulness, taking a peaceful, silent walk in nature, or allowing yourself to take a nap and completely rest your body. Make a commitment to make a daily small step and experience it for seven days. After seven days check in with yourself and notice how you are feeling. Check in with that energy you feel in your body. Are you noticing a difference in your energy? Can you feel it? Self-care is about allowing your body to heal from all the doing and business you identify with. Allow yourself to just be, and your perspective on life will completely change. Journal your observations and take any messages you are hearing.

Chapter 6

The Gift of Healing

When we are in the practice of tapping into our feelings, getting support from a trained healing specialist, and taking small momentum steps forward each day, we get closer and closer to that "self" we have been separated from. Sometimes when we take small steps forward it feels as if nothing is happening. Taking too large a step, though, would eventually shut us down in the energy of overwhelm. This journey doesn't produce immediate tangible evidence, and it's easy to feel like we may as well stop. But healing is a process, and we don't see the results in a big way until we are on the other side.

When I began writing down my progress in my daily journal, I began to see the progress I was making. Consistency and having someone hold us accountable are the most important actions we can take when making any changes in our lives and healing from those old stories from the past that we have identified with for so long.

When we commit to ourselves and heal no matter what the circumstance, we are shown the most beautiful and abundant life. My life used to feel as if I were living in a dense fog, the kind that suddenly drifts in. I couldn't see the road in front of me. I didn't know how far I could go. I didn't know where my road would take me. Healing helped me walk through it, and now I am living on the other side in crystal clarity. All my old beliefs and stories I used to identify with have all turned to light.

Healing Out of a Marriage

Sometimes the healing ultimately begins with letting go. "Feel the discomfort and do it anyway," has been a motto I have followed throughout my healing experience. This makes room by clearing out the old to bring in the new. What I know now is that I had to let go of what I thought was a forever union. I had to let go of what was blocking my inner soul.

My marriage was a place of comfort, loyalty, and trust. We built an incredible life together for thirty years. We raised four amazing children, traveled the world, and lived a materially abundant life. We were not identified with those tangible things, but we were afforded a beautiful family home in Maryland, a home in Puerto Rico, a beach house in Delaware, children in private schools, and a life filled with experiences that some only dream about. The abundance taught me that things are not what make us feel happy.

Before I met my husband, relationships were not working out for me when I was in my twenties. I was unwilling to heal the baggage I carried with me. Exposing it to anyone meant rejection and abandonment, so I covered it with a confident, fake smile. I had convinced myself I was going to be single for the rest of my life. I noticed I was feeling emotions that were foreign to me, and my potential suitors seemed to run in the opposite direction whenever these strange, unearthed emotions came to the surface. Those feelings churned inside of me like a tsunami. The trauma and pain of rejection and insecurities from past relationships felt unmanageable sometimes.

There was even room for a deep trauma of sexual abuse I experienced in Paris when I lived there as a nanny. I had left the security of my family home and ventured off to an unknown place for adventure. I was to stay in France for one year looking after two little boys in the small town of Toulouse. The mother was an artist who spoke only Dutch and French, as did her boys. My high school French failed to help me understand the daily dialect. I did, however, become fluent, especially after drinking the local red wine. I was allowed a month off from my caregiving duties from Floris, age eight, and Peter, age six. They were naughty little boys. They would hide on the top shelf of the wooden armoire giggling hysterically when I couldn't find them. Their manners were impeccable when they sat at the dinner table. Madam would make sure of this by reaching across the table and clunking the tops of their heads with her metal spoon if they spoke out of turn or ate too fast.

I chose my month off to go to Paris and stay with an elderly woman and her daughter. This was a great adventure, and I got to know Paris like it was my hometown. I welcomed the hustle and bustle of city energy.

The countryside in Toulouse was quiet, and the only daily excitement was the farm trucks delivering rolls of golden hay to local hungry cows.

Paris was filled with parties and freedom from any responsibilities. I can remember going to an intimate dinner party at a new friend's home. The host presented dinner to us in a small stewing pot. I was horrified as I opened the lid and saw a whole rabbit cut up in parts and smothered with Dijon mustard. Its head was looking straight up at me. I graciously declined this rather strange delicacy. During my time there no one knew I was an American, as I had acquired the French look as well as the language. My hairstyle back then was short with a long swoosh of hair in the front. My favorite piece of clothing was a vintage fur collar that I would match with everything. It even looked perfect with my brightly colored red lipstick.

Each day I would take out my map—no GPS in those days—and set a course around each arrondissement, or district. With my small, black leather backpack, a bottle of water, and a carefully chosen outfit bought at the local Parisian flea market, I would begin my trek at exactly 9 a.m., stopping only throughout the day for a quick coffee and bread. It was all I could afford, being on a limited salary. I would, of course, pretend to be in abundance of financial flow, as I gazed past the various French clothing and shoe boutiques.

About two weeks into my grand adventure on my own, the day began as all the others did, gathering my backpack, water, outfit, and the map. This day I would be changed forever. My nineteen years of innocence would be damaged by a stranger who somehow lured me into an abandoned building and molested me in an unusable bathroom stall. It happened so fast I didn't know how to react quickly enough. As I stood with my legs wide open, my newly purchased trousers at my ankles, standing on top of the broken toilet seat, I felt helpless as he jammed his grimy, disgusting hand in my vagina. I can remember his fingers feeling cold, and he asked me in his strong French accent if *I liked it*. I don't recall what I said to him as he began unbuckling his own pants.

When I finally found my inner power, I kicked him backward and ran down the winding, cold stairway, past the broken windowpanes and out through the heavy wooden door with the large antique brass doorknob. The outside cold air seemed to wake me up instantly, as I began to run the labyrinth of unfamiliar streets. There was no one there to protect me. There was no one to tell this young girl that everything was going to be okay. I had to bury my fearful trauma deep within me. I remember that horrible life-changing day as if it were yesterday.

Telling anyone would be too embarrassing. *How could you have allowed someone to do that to you? Why didn't you stop him? What were you wearing?* You know, those questions people immediately ask that blame the victim. So I held this story within me and never told a soul until I began my awakening and felt my feelings from the past, thirty years later. No one in my family knew anything about this story. I just recently revealed this trauma to my daughter.

I was attracted to romantic relationships that reflected what I sensed inside. That inner pain followed me everywhere. My inner feelings became my magnet, and those unchartered waters seemed way too deep to dive into. The pain seemed to hush for a little while after experiencing intensive anger therapy, but it only skimmed the surface of my healing.

The baseball bat I used to release my inner pain became my trusted ally and unharnessed my past experiences that had altered my life course. This treatment of therapy was completely new to me. I had never heard of releasing anger by hitting a punching bag with a bat. We would not talk during the session. I would simply release the bottled-up emotions that I had been carrying. At the beginning of the session, I would gently hit the bag with fear of looking completely silly to my therapist. By the end, it felt as if I were being controlled by something else. The rage, the tears, and the aching gushed out of me like a raging Colorado river. I had to sneak to these sessions because my mother forbade me to receive any therapy. She believed it was only for weak people with problems. No child of hers would need any help because our family was tough. A strong cup of Earl Grey tea was a method of healing in my family. I drank a lot of tea! I went anyway. My inner center started to heal just enough to suddenly meet him—my husband.

In a small-town, dimly lit bar in Pennsylvania, I saw my future partner across the room, gently leaning against the wall talking to a mutual friend from high school. He wore a rather unique black trench coat and a black and white checked scarf wrapped around his neck; his hair was shoulder length, carefully combed and looking as if he wanted to make a good impression. In that moment of putting eyes on one another, I knew he was the one—the one with whom I would spend the majority of my adult life.

What I didn't know then was I had brought with me those unhealed deeper emotions into this innocent union. Throughout our union together my patterns would percolate frequently with no safe place for them to land. At those moments I needed a soft touch or a gentle word to help navigate the deeper spirals of pain. That was nowhere to be found. When our four children left the nest, my patterns caught up with me and I began feeling completely out of my alignment. The children were my safe harbor that blinded my reality, and he had his work to hide behind. The constant care of my children's every need was a great distraction to keep me focused away from the trouble brewing.

My then husband, or what I affectionately call him now, my "wasband," was the president of his own company he created in 1993 that has just celebrated its twenty-eighth year in business. I was the CEO (chief executive officer) of my children and my family. I was in charge of transportation to and from their private schools, which were an hour each way. I was in charge of cleaning our large home with nine bedrooms and six bathrooms. The dinner menu was always cooked from scratch with organic ingredients carefully prepared before my drive to the school pick-up lane.

Instead of deeply nurturing myself, I nurtured myself with animals, which I was responsible for each day. We, at one point, opened our home to three dogs, two cats, two miniature donkeys, two ponies, six geese, hamsters, and lizards that I had to feed live crickets to. Yuck! At one point our menagerie included fourteen guinea pigs. I made the mistake of replacing a deceased female guinea pig with what I thought was another female. This male was set loose into the cage with the three other unassuming females. Later that month, I opened the cage for their morning feeding and I thought I was hallucinating, as there in the cage were twelve babies. It may have been easier to receive more therapy than to fill my pain with yet another animal.

We tried everything within the confines of togetherness to make the institution of marriage work. The children were the glue that bound us together in the beginning. That grip became less secure as we came to the end of our path together.

Throughout my marriage I was always interested in my personal growth, reading every self-help book new to the shelves of my favorite bookstore. The stories always seemed to resonate with what I was experiencing. It wasn't until I began studying my patterns that I began to understand that the little voice inside of me was calling out to expand into who I was. I would not settle for less than what I deserved.

My husband was a loyal provider I could count on for anything tangible in my family's life, but the emotional support was something a bit out of balance. I needed to be supported emotionally. I needed to express my emotions. I needed someone to gently take my hand and assure me that everything was going to be alright. I craved that as a child, and I searched for it in my marriage. I never found it.

After many years of tearful arguments full of frustration, I began feeling in my gut that this familiar union was becoming untethered. The children were all living their own lives now, and we were left with one another. The fear I carried with me that we would grow apart was now coming true. We were energetically coming apart at the seams.

I remember sitting in my living room surrounded by my antique treasures I had collected during our life together. Those antique Chinese chairs I had inherited, the dark wooden pool table that was only used during the holidays, the gold gilded mirror that hung above the fireplace, and the mahogany side table that belonged to my mother when my parents lived in Hong Kong, became my comfort. As I sat weeping on my red velvet sofa, I realized my marriage was over. I finally had the courage to end this union that was my forever—the union that now I would have to grieve.

I do not recommend the leaving part. On the other side of the leaving are many other challenges that some of us are not ready for when we make a hasty departure in fear rather than in a place of love. I do recommend listening to the inner voice when it whispers, "The time is right now to spiritually grow." I finally listened to her, and another layer of healing began.

The Gift of Healing Allowed Me to Do This

The ending of my marital union seemed so clear when the time became right. Taking that leap into fearful darkness felt like I had let go of weight I had been carrying for many years. With a heavy, deep, inner sigh as we held tight to one another, tears streaming down our faces, we lovingly agreed to try the separation for a short time to see how we felt. In the past we would respond to one another in anger. My husband would say, "I'm done" and walk quickly out the door only to return after his temper and frustration had settled. The practice of taking small steps was useful even here.

It was a cold February day. I packed my temporary suitcase filled with sentimental possessions and drove to our home in another state. I was free. I was ready to discover the other side of my fear. What I didn't know was my fear would take another form. I had never lived independently all my life. In my late teens and until I met my husband, I was emotionally and physically taking care of my mother, who suffered from her own marital heartbreak and financial ruin. Her unhealed pain became mine, as she struggled to pay her bills and make her move back to her native England to live in a small quaint town in Wiltshire. The image of her standing in her jean skirt and comfortable cotton shirt, holding her beloved dog, Bean, in front of her tiny cottage with wisteria growing over the door, will be etched in my mind forever.

The newness of my transformation was about to look me directly in the eye. I didn't know this woman on her own—in charge of her own finances, believing in herself, writing books, growing her coaching practice, and deciding how to renovate her bathrooms in her beloved beach house in Rehoboth Beach. Feeling into this unknown person who was finally speaking loud enough to be heard by herself was so foreign. This stranger was a woman who went from looking after her mother to meeting her potential husband and getting married. Although she was comfortable being alone, she never made her own decisions about money, owning a home, or at the least, paying rent. She relied on others to take care of her needs.

The Love of Uncoupling Rather Than the Agony of Divorce

The pain and trauma we decide to hold on to can alter the way we perceive the ending of relationships. Our society only views divorce as one sided. We ultimately give control of the emotional course to a stranger. Divorce attorneys seem to rub their hands together with glee, when another couple cuts the bond of their coveted togetherness. The way we end any relationship is up to us, and sometimes the negative drama is driven by that unleashed and unhealed pain from our past.

My *"wasband"* and I have chosen a path that not many who leave a long-term union experience. We are creating a new union separately with love, honor, and respect. We are loving one another despite the differences in our relationship. Our main concern is how our children see us in this new place. The constant that they knew all their lives has changed, so keeping the relationship as loving as possible will allow the transition to be less painful. I don't want to assume they don't have pain, and I will honor them and allow them to express any emotions that come up. Our intention is to show them that love has a new energy even when we live in two different states and have two new relationships. There could be many reasons to take the route of anger, resentment, blaming, and hatred, but this energy would ultimately affect ourselves.

Disease could show up in my body. I could live again in that fog that was full of negative energy. We are choosing to uncouple our way. We are creating this non-union with each other filled with support, love, friendship, fairness, and communication. All the healing I have experienced has allowed me to not hold on to any of those old stories and react with those painful emotions. The idea of what we focus on or feel inwardly is what we ideally attract. Of course, I have experienced a tremendous amount of grief and sadness in this uncoupling, but I know what tools to use to heal those feelings and ultimately let them go. I have cried so many tears and I have allowed myself to grieve the loss of what once was. My practice of clearing, healing, and letting go has been a welcomed ally whenever I need to move through pain. Feeling the sensation that arises in my body and understanding the story associated with it, is now my daily practice. When we allow ourselves to feel that discomfort, that's when we can heal and ultimately let go for good.

When we heal ourselves and don't throw the blame onto others who may have caused pain, we are able to live a more peaceful and loving life. I will continue to live in this energy to show the next generation how to live in a healthy way.

Here Is What You Can Do

I know divorce is not something any of us want if we have entered this sacred union, but if you are one who has begun the uncoupling process, here are some steps I experienced to make the process more loving:

Step 1 - Finding Emotional Freedom

Letting go of anger and unhappiness with your former partner is the first step in conscious uncoupling. Reacting to negative emotions is a choice. Freeing yourself from the burden of negative energy can promote the positive outlook you need to achieve success after your marriage is over. Being conscious of the heavy energy can free you from the emotional attachment.

Step 2 - Reclaiming Your Personal Power

In a marriage, we can adapt to the needs and expectations of our partners. Understanding where you may have given your power away in the marriage will lead you to connect with yourself again. Recognizing your discomfort when someone speaks to you and listening to how you respond can help you to change how you react in a more powerful way.

Step 3 - Breaking Negative Patterns

Rewrite those repetitive negative patterns. Take out a journal and write down those old stories that repeat themselves over and over. Begin reframing a better story and create better patterns of behavior. Breaking patterns of behavior that do not lead to good results is a practical way to learn and grow from your breakup. Positive energy will start to be more of a part of your life.

Step 4 - Building Your Own Happily Ever After

Determine what your ideal life will be and begin working toward your own happiness even after your divorce is finalized. Live your life as if it's already happening the way you imagined. Try and surround yourself with a circle of friends who will support this vision with you.

How It Changes the World

When we begin to heal the energy from the quiet center of ourselves, we change and heal the world around us. Those people closest to us begin to change. Who they are connected to begins to change and so on and so on. When we heal ourselves, we heal the children of the world—not necessarily our biological children, but the children of the world.

First, we get to take the steps to soothe the pain in ourselves, then that new and healthy inner frequency vibrates on the outside. Remember, what we are feeling inwardly is our magnet to what and whom we attract. In my coaching, some of my clients come to me trying to change the behaviors of others around them, thinking that will change who they are. I assure them that others will mirror what they are feeling. I have witnessed this shift in marriages, with their children, in their workplaces, and in manifestation. Change the energy you vibrate into the world, and you will change how others vibrate to you. It happens every time.

Chapter 7

When We Heal—
Heal Yourself,
Heal Your
Children

"In the absence of reflection, history often repeats itself...
Research has clearly demonstrated that our children's
attachment to us will be influenced by what happened to
us when we were young if we do not come to process and
understand those experiences."
—Dan Siegel-Clinical Professor of Psychiatry

Breaking the Cycle

When we become aware of our own inner patterns, we can understand who may be running the show. The little girl or boy inside of us who only knows the patterns from the past will be the one who guides us—that little one who feels the fear, anger, guilt, or resentment inherited from a past generation. Remember, we hold on to that past from three generations in our DNA, as I quoted in Chapter Two. My inner child wished she had known then what she knows now. She wished someone would have made her feel special. She wished she was told that she was enough exactly the way she wanted to be. Even with this illusion of who I thought I was, I broke the pattern I had been carrying most of my life. Our children can be our greatest teachers of healing.

Raising my four children was my test. Even though I was spiritually asleep as a young mother, I somehow didn't pass on my painful patterns of the past. There was a sense that a force was guiding me to raise them in a different way. The force was my inner voice asking me to take care of her. I became that little girl again, giving her what she craved as a child. I was somehow able to steer my children away from the pain and trauma she had experienced. Oh, I am sure there were a few patterns that slipped by, but I created a life for my children that I wished I had experienced. The ability to be free from the constraints of what someone thought I should be or what I should have, liberated my children to live a life of choice. In a recent conversation, my eldest son commented that it felt really good to be able to choose the path of his own life. As an adult, I began to understand that I could give to myself what I didn't receive from others.

A perfect example of giving myself what I wanted was wrapped around my birthday. In my own childhood, I can remember waiting every year for that birthday surprise party, convincing myself that this would be that year. I would wake up before sunrise with exuberant excitement, only ending the day with disappointment. Every year I had the same fantasy of how my birthday would unfold. I would be secretly taken away for a few hours with my mom, pretending to stall, while everyone gathered at home, hiding thousands of colorful balloons. Paper streamers would be hanging from every corner of our house. My friends from school and from my riding would hide themselves behind sofas and in closets, quietly waiting to jump out and scream, "Surprise!"

My mother did her best to acknowledge my special day, but the reality was I would choose my birthday dinner menu, unwrap my gifts with my parents, brother, and sister at the old wooden dining room table, and then I would return to my room and wait for the next year. In that moment I remember feeling disappointment and guilt—disappointment that the reality of my birthday had ended the same way, but also guilt for even asking for more. How dare I want more than what was given to me! "Sarah don't be ungrateful," I was told.

As an adult, I took charge of what I wanted to experience as a child. I would throw myself birthday parties. These weren't just any parties with hot dogs on the grill, paper plates, and cold beer. These were parties adorned with fragrant, colorful flowers I picked from my garden, tablescapes designed as if royalty was attending, and small niches that echoed the chosen international theme and delectable food carefully created ahead of time by me—chicken tikka masala, vast pots of flavorful stews, and roasted vegetables flavored with the latest Italian spice. Huge, white tents were set up outside in our generous backyard under ancient oak trees that had never seen such activities. They seemed to want to be a part of the fun.

Every August, in the depths of Maryland humidity, I would begin the process of my creation. I chose a different theme each year, and I would spend weeks creating the perfect scene.

My fortieth birthday party was one that stands out in my mind. The theme was Morocco. I used a small room in my house and recreated the look of a traditional Persian harem. I remember hearing gasps of excitement when the guests arrived. The room that normally was a place where they sat drinking wine quietly by the stone fireplace, was now decorated to reflect a mysteriously exotic room for concubines. The ceilings of this room were draped with silk and satin fabric, layer upon layer. Every inch of the furniture and walls was covered with bright red, pink, orange, and yellow fabric. The whole room was transformed into a page fresh out of a Middle Eastern tourist magazine. Even the outside echoed the theme of the indoor room. The outdoor tables were covered with the same yellow, orange, and red silk fabric, and the flowers seemed to speak the same language. I wore a black and silver traditional belly dancing outfit that jingled with every move. I even had a chef create a white Buddha cake. At the end of all the laborious decorating and before all the guests would arrive, I secretly stood in silence and just smiled for what I had just created and offered to myself. My birthday experiences were choreographed from a place that was never filled in my younger days.

My children's birthday parties were filled with that same spirited play, creativity, and love. I gifted myself my children's lives. The idea was born in my mind, and then the most magnificent birthday celebrations were created for my four children.

One party is etched in my mind. It was my daughter's fifth birthday. We had just moved into our dream house overlooking the banks of the Bohemia River, which flows into the vast Chesapeake Bay. It was a perfect setting for the idea percolating in my mind.

I had begun thinking of ideas for a magical Cinderella party for my daughter, Fiona, weeks before that scheduled date. This was not the commercialized type of Cinderella. This was to be my own version. What I didn't know was the previous owners had left their white horse-drawn carriage in our new barn. The carriage looked as if Cinderella herself had just stepped off to meet her Prince Charming at the ball. This perfect detail led to my creative magic.

I had arranged that the previous owner's farm hand would be the driver of the carriage on the day of celebration. He was to wear his black tuxedo, and his head would be adorned by his satin top hat. The two chestnut horses left on our property would be strapped into the leather harnesses.

Before my daughter's little friends arrived, I painted the small white pumpkins carefully with gold paint. Our whole house seemed to sparkle with magic. Candy sticks were placed beside each pumpkin on the table, which was draped with a silver tablecloth. When instructed, the little guests, dressed in their favorite party dresses, waved their candy sticks over their golden pumpkins in hopes of the promised surprise to appear. When they opened their eyes, they were led outside where the white carriage and the beautifully groomed horses were standing. Screams of excitement erupted as they were escorted onto a carriage for a ride around the lawn. I remember feeling as excited as the children, reliving with them what I never experienced.

Each one of my four children was allowed to bloom into their own person. There was a moment I thought continuing the riding saga was going to be a part of all my children's lives. I did take my daughter, Fiona, for a short time to some horse shows and pony club events, but something was beginning to feel out of alignment. That familiar feeling of judgment and impatience bubbled up when my daughter turned into the wrong jump and tumbled to the ground. There was that pattern I inherited. It was trying to tell me something.

I tried to do the same with my son, Avery. He didn't want to have any part of riding when one day he dismounted and walked into the house, throwing his black riding hat to the ground. As he retreated to the house at age four, he said, "I don't want to do this anymore, Mommy." The little girl inside of me seemed to jump for joy that Avery was able to decide for himself. A sense of peace filled my body, even though he was breaking my identified pattern. After this realization, the ponies lived out their lives frolicking in our green pastures surrounding our home.

I witnessed my children's passions for surfing, animals, and a love for anything fast + furious. My youngest had a passion for race cars. My three boys and one girl grew up pursuing four different interests even though what they chose was not something I understood or agreed to. I remember the scene of my three boys in our three-car garage one day with their dad. The pungent smell of exhaust from the engines and worktables, strewn with nuts and bolts, became a haven for the engineering minds. Their dad was explaining to them how a specific motor worked. Two of my three boys focused on every intricate detail of how the engine worked. One of my sons watched a noisy fly buzzing in the window, desperately trying to find a safe passage to the outside. In the stories below you will understand who that child was.

As their mom, I stood back and gently guided them to their own passions. Oh, how I wish I was given that gift.

Surfing and being surrounded by water was what my oldest son, Julian, chose to pursue. I was always amazed that this shy little boy who was afraid to ask to use the bathroom in kindergarten, ended up loving a sport that requires not just skill, but bravery. This was his passion, even though engineering is his day-to-day job working at the family business in the small town of Haure de Grace, Maryland. Moving to and living in California after college was how he was able to surf every day after work. The Pacific Ocean became his refuge to his inner peace and calm, even when he occasionally spotted sharks swimming underneath his surfboard. These sightings would have made me quickly walk across the water to the nearest shoreline. Julian just exhaled until the next wave swelled.

Each of our family vacations were experienced around water, from Costa Rica to Australia. He would bring his brightly colored surfboards, wrapped in plastic bubbles, ready to test out the unknown waters of our family vacation. All of his siblings would have to squeeze into the corners of our large SUV (Sports Utility Vehicle) to accommodate Julian's passion. His side job is his surfboard company, Posteur, just outside of Philadelphia. With his gray and white Newfoundland dog, Newton, at his feet, he shapes various boards for many surfing enthusiasts all over the world. Julian has grown from a shy little boy to an adventurous young man traveling the world with his trusted surf boards. Mexico was his latest adventure, where he shared a room with not only his trio of surfing buddies, but with a rather large tarantula.

My daughter, Fiona, decided to end her career as a rider when I recognized that my old patterning was beginning to take over. She instead had an insatiable passion for animals. We constantly were making trips to the SPCA, Society for the Protection of Cruelty of Animals, to adopt another pet. Dogs and cats were what she always convinced me that our family needed. I gave in every time. She was a great nurturer to those animals that were less fortunate. Even with her petite frame, she was a great force and advocate for creatures less fortunate.

One rescue was one of my favorites. An innocent venture turned out to change our family's lives forever. Windsor the dog was vast. He was black and enormous and barely fit in my car. He was cross-eyed and ran laterally because his legs were too long for his body. He was one year old and had everything wrong with him. He had gangly, long legs, crossed eyes, a large birthmark patch on the left side of his shoulder, and an ear that stood tall while the other drooped limply. He was a mess, but Fiona was determined to make him part of our family menagerie. He turned out to be one of our biggest joys, and we all loved him for the very short time he lived on Earth.

The other dogs that were part of our family at the time seemed to roll their eyes at us when this massive, black intruder entered their quiet sanctuary. His life was cut short after only two years with us. He ended up with terrible heart disease and died one night with a great thump on the floor. His life was to teach all of us how to celebrate each day even

if life is short. Fiona was determined to give a better life to him and all
the other rescues. To this day, her biggest love of her life, other than her
long-term boyfriend, is a dog. Eddie has won her heart. He is a very large
Bernese Mountain dog who joined her family during COVID and now
lives in her large twenty-sixth floor apartment in Chicago.

Our third son, Avery, was that child who spoke up for himself, declared
he didn't want to ride, and pursued his own passion for music. Even though
my oldest and youngest boys followed in the footsteps of their engineer
father, this child was determined to live a life that resonated with him. He
was the one watching the buzzing fly in the garage while his brothers and
Dad had their heads under the hood of another car.. To this day he thrives
in a world dating back to the 1970s. From his long, Jim Morrison-style
hair to his light blue French Citron with the blue checked gingham seats,
he sets the tone with how he decided to live.

The third floor with the haunted room was transformed into a record-
ing studio. He chose the room that was supposedly filled with our resident
ghost. She was the wife that had been pushed down the winding stairs of
the foyer to never be seen alive again. Her spirit was seen by only a chosen
few. Stories are told that her body was buried in the archives beneath the
veranda that wrapped around the green-painted porch outside. Her spirit
resided in the room that became his music studio.

Avery and the other three children confessed they saw shadows and
heard heavy footsteps while they tried to sleep. Each wall of this room
was covered in soundproof foam, so everyone down below would be
spared the noise of the electric bass guitars and the drums played by
other members of his small garage band he created. The foam he used
did not work. We heard every note. Everything was about music. He
would practice endless piano chords over and over again on our baby
grand piano. There was even a time when he taught himself how to play
the Indian zither—that rectangular stringed instrument played on one's
lap. The wailing sound of this unique wooden sound box filled the quiet

of our house until one of his siblings shouted from the first floor, "Avery, can you stop that noise!"

My youngest son, who is the tallest of them all, is living his dream and drives for a Hyundai race team. His six-foot, one-inch lean body fits perfectly into the tight squeeze of the car's cockpit. "Race Car Rory," as his friends affectionately call him, is all about anything with a motor. He spent all of his waking hours in the garage with his dad, taking apart and rebuilding engines from any vehicle that had four wheels. He began his passion for the hum of load engines with go-karting—not the soap box version like in Boy Scouts, but a version of low-to-the-ground machines that travel way too fast around a track. I always joked that it was a great way for me to lose weight. Watching my young son drive at ninety miles per hour would make my stomach turn in circles. Each weekend during the season, he and his dad would travel across the country to compete with other go-kart drivers from around the world. He excelled in his sport because he wanted to experience it. I was never on the sidelines telling him what to do and how to do it. He decided for himself.

Watching my children discover their own passions made that little girl inside of me feel calm and so proud. It was as if this pride were being reflected back to her.

When We Heal, We Show the World a Mirror

"If there is to be healing in the world, there needs to be healing in the nations. If there is to be healing in the nations, there needs to be healing in the cities. If there is to be healing in the cities, there needs to be healing with our neighbors. If there is to be healing with our neighbors, there needs to be healing in the home. If there is to be healing in the home, there needs to be healing in the heart."
—Davidji, Meditation teacher

This quote has been a quiet reminder that, to this day, I live by. All that arises comes from within all of us. When we heal ourselves, we heal the children of our world. It all begins with us to change and heal the world as we know it. Future generations will be forever changed.

We all have healing to do. If we didn't, we wouldn't be here. We grow up with humans for teachers. These people (parents, guardians, teachers, siblings, etc.) are imperfect. Since we can only give who we are, people affect us differently based on where they are on their own spiritual paths.

When we set out to do the most rewarding work of our lives—healing our old wounds—we cultivate less fear and more love, peace, joy, and self-forgiveness, which leads to better self-care and personal choices. All of this becomes who we are. This, in turn, is who we give to others. Unfortunately, who the world sees is the unhealed part of ourselves. The discomfort of what we need to face is somehow buried or pushed away, hoping that it will never resurface again. But it does, over and over again. The world is full of people who are unaware of themselves and their wounds, so they just keep reacting to everything in a knee-jerk kind of way which perpetuates all of our problems.

When we give ourselves an authentically joyful, peaceful way, how we treat all others (including humans, animals, nature, and the planet we are so dependent upon for survival) becomes peaceful and filled with love and compassion. This leads easily to forgiveness, service to others, and better choices for all.

When this kind of energy is put into motion, it can and does affect, not just our immediate surroundings like our home lives, neighborhoods, and communities, but also the whole rest of the world. This has been finally proven by science. The ripple effect is real. When we set anything into motion (a thought, word, or action) it is like throwing a stone into a still pond. When the stone pierces the surface of the water, it creates ripples that extend from the entry point in concentric circles in all directions. We don't realize how much of the world we affect every day.

This effect goes far beyond those we come in contact with. Its reach is infinite.

This Is What Happens When You Heal

When one of my beloved clients first began working with me, she was experiencing deep inner turbulence with her mother. She was stressed, had no confidence, and no boundaries. She would feel triggered by the words and actions of her mother, whom she believed had not loved or respected her for sixty years. Every time they spoke on the phone each morning, her mother would ask, "How's your weight?" This created shame and anger energy within her. Her mother's own pain became her own.

Those outdated beliefs she was still identifying with needed an upgrade. The first step I encouraged her to begin practicing was meditation. She had never used meditation to quiet herself. She began to be aware of her inner narrative and hear the thoughts she was believing were real. She even began to detach from the emotions that her thoughts were creating. Her inner narrative shifted from, *I am not enough, I am not worthy, I am not loved,* to *I am worthy, I deserve to be treated with love, I am open to receiving.* I would remind her that her thoughts were creating her reality.

Over the course of nine months, she felt more confident to set boundaries with her mother. She set the tone and expectation in her home before anyone arrived for family gatherings. This was a powerful tool that set the stage for anyone trying to bring drama into her now peaceful sanctuary. The triggers began to disappear. She was able to feel more peace and calm. She even noticed that her newfound energy was changing the energy of her mother and other family members who were the source of her old stories. What we focus on inside of us is what we attract. She believes now that she is the "goddess matriarch of her family, standing firmly in her pillar of light". That is who she has become, and so it is!

The Golden Light Meditation

*Take a moment here to drop into your quiet center. Bring
your focus to your breath. Begin to inhale deeply into your
beautiful body calm, peaceful energy. Now exhale slowly all the
thoughts you want to let go. Breathe in calm, peaceful energy.
Exhale what wants to go. Notice your body relaxing here.
Your shoulders are dropped. Your jaw is unclenched. Feel the
heaviness in your body being supported on your chair.*

*I invite you now to bring your focus to the very top of your
head. At this very tip see a large golden ball of light. This ball
is so bright and shiny and full of healing powers. See your
head's crown opening and inviting the golden ball of light to
begin traveling down the inner center of your body—through
your throat, down your chest, through your stomach, your
pelvis, down your legs and into your feet, through every cell,
vessel, muscle, and bone along the way. Fill your body with
this golden transforming energetic light. You are feeling the
warmth of the light as it travels down through you to the roots
of Mother Earth. Feel your body come alive with this magnetic
charge from Divine light. Rest here for a few breaths, noticing
how differently you feel. Trust that you are experiencing this,
affirming that when you open your eyes, this is what you will
feel in the present moment!*

*When you are ready and have decided, begin rubbing your
hands together. Once you feel warm energy between your
hands, gently place your hands over your eyes and allow your
eyes to gently open.*

Chapter 8

Your
Healing Style

Your Inner Energy Reflects Your Outer Style

Clothes and style have always been an integral part of my life. Being conscious of how I presented myself to the outside world has been an important part of my growth. My mother was in that generation of dressing up and looking respectable even on an airplane, that time when it was a treat to be able to fly the friendly skies. I can remember waiting in line on standby for the cheapest flight to be offered to us as we awaited the long trip to England for our summer holiday. I looked perfectly put together even when I had to find a place to sleep on the bare, airport floors, in my matching blue and white floral dress and perfectly polished blue patent leather shoes.

Fashion and looking presentable were more important than comfort. My identity was wrapped in this gift from my mother. She would dress me. She would decide what we were to wear to various dinner parties with her friends or if we were to host a holiday party at our house on Copeland School Road. I never established my own style. It was always the style expected by my mother rather than created by me.

As a teen I can remember trying to look like my sister. She dressed in that preppy style of the seventies. I thought that was me. My sister protected her clothes under lock and key. She padlocked her room before she left for school so her little sister couldn't help herself to her beloved argyle sweaters and the pants with blue lily pads. I, of course, found a way to borrow her clothes each morning and then return them before she came home from her day at school.

My plan failed when she unexpectedly came home early from high school. I walked into the kitchen and there I was, caught red-handed by my sister with every thread belonging to her. My secret escapades were revealed.

Even when my sister left for college, the door was padlocked. My mom would send adoring photos of me to Charlotte at her private college in Middleburg, Virginia. We'd receive frantic phone calls with my sister screaming at my mother, as I was captured modeling her entire wardrobe. Head to toe, I would wear everything my sister didn't want me to wear.

I was always searching for validation from others, wearing clothes I thought would get attention. I never really established my own unique style until I healed my old identity and began vibrating to my own frequency. The breakthrough that I feel now is this inner feeling of flow and ease. My inner feeling now matches my outer style. My calm and relaxed inner center is reflected in my relaxed, boho style. I wear colors and patterns that feel relaxed and gently shape my five-foot, four-inch muscular frame. No more searching for validation from others. No more squeezing into clothes that are too tight or that would please others. I set the tone of my individual style. It feels as if I am Cinderella, and I am finally fitting into the right shoe.

Clutter Is Not Just Stuff

The sacred spaces we surround ourselves with are areas that expose what we are feeling on the inside and mirror the thoughts we identify with. The old programming that appears in our outer environment is a direct reflection of our identity. Our outer appearance or style is one area, but our environment we live in has the same energetic vibration. Our minds can be the narrative of what our environment looks like. If we are consumed with the clutter of thoughts, our outer environment tends to look the same.

When our family moved into our beloved home in Chesapeake City, Maryland in 2000, my mind was in a very confused and disorganized place. My outer environment reflected just that. I remember painting my walls in every room dark blue. My inner darkness was revealed on the walls of our beautiful house. There were piles of papers that needed to be filed and old family heirlooms that were broken or damaged, but I felt guilty for getting rid of them.

If there was an empty space, there was something in it. I was not cemented into my own inner sacred space. I was still hanging on to those old memories of my mom, thinking her style was mine. The picture of her bedroom still resonates with what I thought was my vibration. Endless piles of newspapers were stacked in various corners of her bedroom. She couldn't throw anything away and she didn't. Her closet was jammed with clothes that were never worn. These clothes hung with the tags still attached. The idea of buying something sent her into a panic of guilt. She once told me the reason she kept the tags on was to calm her guilt, knowing she could always return *them*. Those old beliefs that she wasn't even worthy enough to have something new, haunted her throughout life.

Sacred space design is one of my favorite things to create for others. First, I work with clients on clearing out the thoughts that stop them from connecting to themselves. It is kind of like inner housekeeping. I help them step into that inner room in their heads, take that imaginary golden broom, and sweep those old, limited thoughts down into an imaginary drain that is connected to Mother Earth. This visualization helps with the letting go process. Our thoughts can be the clutter that block us from the clarity and manifestation in our lives. One of the happiest revelations for me has been the understanding that the limited old stories I believed were all lies.

Once our inner space is cleared out, we begin the process of reconnection—reconnection to the truth of who we are born to be, which is all we seek . . . the love and peace that we want. The abundance we want is already within us. It is our birthright. After this work and once my clients feel realigned, I can then design the space that best reflects this new energy.

I went from dark blue walls with clutter to clean, fresh white walls with organized spaces. There is balance. There is comfort. There is a home that can be easily translated. My outer style is in alignment with how I am feeling inside. My home now feels as if you are walking into a tranquil spa. It gently whispers calm in every corner. White walls, white furniture, live green plants, cozy blankets on a cold winter's day, and collections of Buddhas await anyone who enters this sacred healing sanctuary of my inner being. My clients who come in for an energy clearing session of anyone experiencing my manifesting retreats, never want to leave.

Here's How to Begin Clearing Your Outer Space

Like anything we do in our lives, taking small but measurable steps is the way to start the process. When our environmental space needs attention, start first with something manageable. First, start with a junk drawer. You know that drawer with all the things you tell yourself you will use one day: the rubber bands, the nail files, the small little charm from your child's bracelet, and the pens that don't work anymore. Just start there. The after-tidy feeling in your body will inspire you to take an even bigger step.

A strategy I offer to my clients when I have a large decluttering project is to set a kitchen timer and only reorganize for that designated time. Start with fifteen minutes and do only that. Add more time and a new project the next day. This is the method of the stepping stones. Take one step at a time to get to the other side.

The last magical trick I want to offer you is to spend a few minutes visualizing the room. My clients take a moment and look at their space. How do they want the room to reflect themselves? What are the most essential pieces in it? What things don't bring them joy? Once they have visualized how they want the room to look and figured out what is essential, they can lovingly begin the process of letting go of what no longer serves this new version of themselves.

This Is What Can Happen When You Heal

Another favorite client of mine just went through this process of self-discovery. The identity and feeling he had about himself was mirrored in his outer environment. The lack and scarcity could be seen in every corner.

When we began working together, Bruce lived in a tiny room he shared with two other renters. The scarcity he felt inside aligned with his outer environment. After his divorce, he was left with nothing. At one point he was even living in his old Volvo. He was at rock bottom and didn't even believe he deserved anything nice. The emptiness of his inner soul was reflected in the inside of his empty car. His divorce took his life out of him, and he blamed himself for the ending.

This was a man who had lived a materialistically abundant life. He made a successful career as a lawyer, built a seven-figure business from scratch, had his two girls in private schools, owned houses in Anguilla, and had two properties at the beaches in Delaware. Even though in his marriage he had all the things that most people dream about having, he was completely emotionally disconnected.

The scarcity he felt seemed to follow him everywhere, and he didn't know where to turn until he began working with me. I took him through the inner work I have taken you through in the earlier chapters. Identifying family patterns and clearing scarcity limitations and beliefs from his mindset were the first steps. Even after months of weekly sessions, his old patterning was beginning to shift but he still lived in the small space cramped with piles of boxes heaped in the corner. His outer environment was not congruent with his new inner energy. I asked him if he was ready to align his inner and outer sacred spaces. With a bright and calm smile, he nodded his head and agreed.

He recently moved to an abundantly spacious apartment. The newly painted white walls of this roomy apartment were ready to welcome him. We began filling the space with a bright blue velvet sofa with dark red satin pillows. The warm wooden floors that are brightly polished are gently covered with the family's Turkish rugs. The lineage of his Farsi upbringing is echoed on the walls by his heirloom calligraphy paintings that were hidden in a closet. His childhood was celebrated with his Hot Wheel cars now sitting on a shelf. He remembers how they brought him joy when he was a child. That same spirit came to life when we were co-creating at my favorite local antique shop. I witnessed him light up when he found an old tennis racket with his birthplace of Forest Hill, NY, written on the old handle. The happy time of his youth playing tennis was remembered and revered.

Comfort and organization are the energies you feel as you take the steep climb up the squeaky steps to the second floor. The windows are generous with light coming from a beautiful park across the street. The shrieks of children playing echo each afternoon when school has finished for the day. He lights his candles each morning to remind himself to be present. He sits each morning and journals his thoughts so he can understand how to feel those once uncomfortable emotions. With my reassurance and weekly accountability sessions, he knows that support is only a phone call away. The change that has occurred in his life is absolutely remarkable. I feel a sense of pride that his inner environment now echoes in his new sacred space. When I see any of my clients find their own light, it confirms to me that anything is possible.

Room In Your Head Meditation

Sit comfortably and just begin bringing your focus to your breath, noticing the coolness as you breathe in and the warmth as you breathe out. Take a few moments to calm and connect.

Begin by rubbing those two spots on the side of your head . . . just gently start messaging those spots. These spots are your temples and between them is your temple . . . your sacred space of awareness. Are you aware of what's happening or are you just the effects of what is happening? How many of your thoughts are you deciding to have and how many are you believing to have? Notice if there are thoughts coming up. If there is, just send a clearing breath to that place. You can't do this if you are thinking of the things you have to finish after this session. Just smile at them and come back to the here and now . . . and focus on the breath again . . . and just allow your thoughts to enter, affirming that those thoughts are just thoughts and nothing else. The magic of thoughts is to not make meaning or judgment about them. Just let them be what they are and maybe become the watcher. Notice that thoughts create the clutter in your sacred mind space. What meaning are you making about them? Are you believing in what you notice, or are you allowing them just to come into your head and then out again? We are going to explore this space.

We are going to go on a little vacation to a sacred space—this space is so relaxing . . . so peaceful and calm—but there may be some things we need to unpack before we get there.

I want you to imagine being in the inside of your head as if it were a room—maybe even see yourself stepping into your head

or the room in your head. Maybe there is a ladder to a door
that opens to the inside. See yourself stepping inside. You're
inside now. As you take a soft, calming breath, be there, look
around. What do you see? Is this space messy and cluttered or is
it clean and organized? What's in there? What are you noticing
in your head space? What is this space you have stepped into?
Is it a large warehouse, a small office, maybe a peaceful yoga
studio? You don't have to create the room. I want to just go into
the center and see what it looks like.

Take a moment and look around. Are there pictures on the
wall or trash on the floor? Is the space too small or too big? Is it
noisy or quiet? No judgment here, just curiosity. Get a sense of
it. Is it brightly lit or kind of dark? Every day we have so many
thoughts going through our minds. These thoughts begin filling
our space. Our minds get so noisy, so cluttered. Let's just start to
change this space, change the energy . . . kind of feng shui our
minds. Let's clean it up. How do you want to make it better?
Anything you no longer want to have in your space, let it go.
Anything you no longer feel connected to, let it go. Maybe there
are some old paintings or broken furniture that no longer excite
you. Let them go. See yourself making a huge pile of unwanted
things and put them in the center of your room in the center of
your head. Anything you want to let go of that no longer serves
your sacred space, toss it in the pile. Just clean it up. Be playful
in your head. Just have fun. There is no right or wrong way.
You are making space for the new.

Are you noticing any more clutter? Toss anything into the pile.
The clutter can also be your thoughts. They can be your words.
Put it all in that pile in the center of your head. Clean it up.

I invite you now to see a golden drain in the center of your room in your head. We are now going to sweep and flush all those thoughts and all your clutter down this drain. This beautiful drain goes all the way down to the ground, travels through to Mother Earth, through all the roots of the plants and trees. Don't worry, everything in the room in your head turns to dust and fertilizes the earth.

There in the corner in the room of your head is a wide, heavy broom. You see yourself picking it up and you begin sweeping your pile of old stuff, those old thoughts in the drain, gently sweeping and flushing all that clutter and stuff to the wide-open golden drain.

As you watch your heavy clutter being sucked down the drain, you feel a sense of lightness in your head, in your body, as you witness what you have been holding on to flush down your golden drain in the room in your head.

Just take a moment here to feel the lightness in your body. See yourself standing in the center of your head. The walls are bare, maybe they are painted all white. It feels fresh. It feels light. It feels clear. As you take a beautiful, deep breath in and exhale, I invite you to see yourself now sitting on a soft white cushion in the center of your head. You feel that peaceful energy in your entire body from the top of your head all the way through to the tips of your toes. It feels so good to be so clear. When we are clear and peaceful on the inside, we attract clarity and peace from the outside. In this new sacred space in the room in your head, you know you can come here anytime you want and clean it out. You can return here whenever you want, whenever you feel the heaviness of life clutter. Let's take one more deep cleansing breath. Rub your hands together, creating warm energy. Place your hands gently over your eyes and fold your eyes open. Now, come back into the present moment.

Chapter 9

Teach Our Children Well

Our children are our future. This can also mean the inner child within us. The way we decide to raise that child within us will affect how we raise that child we have given birth to or the one we may come in contact within our lives. How will they become that future if they are continuing the same patterns that we, as parents, are still holding on to? We get to dive deep into healing ourselves in order to shift the energy in our own children as well as the energy in the world. Helping our children recognize that what they are feeling is perfect will be a first step to breaking the invisible thread to the past. When we don't even know what feelings are, how do we teach our children to recognize their own?

The best results come from a solid space from the parents. We have termed this conscious parenting. Your inner child and someone else's child will reflect your energy.

This Is How We Help Them and Ourselves

Help your child recognize what an emotion feels like. Have them first sit quietly. Invite them to focus on their breathing. Ask them where they are feeling a sensation in their body. Then have them describe this sensation. Allow them to be as descriptive in their own language as possible. They could even use some crayons to describe them. Once they have become familiar with whatever it is that is showing up, you can offer the following tools. Not only can our children benefit by using these tools but we, as adults, can practice them daily when our own emotions should arise. We can even use these practices when we are not in an emotionally charged state, so that we are cemented in a peaceful, calm state.

Dandelioning - To Help Navigate Anger

This first tool I will share with you helped my children understand the sensation of anger. The emotion of anger can be terrifying when the jolt of energy begins to bubble up and takes over their little bodies. Some children don't know what to do or how to control anger.

My middle son used this tool many times as he was in tune with feeling emotional charges when he didn't like something that was happening to him. I can remember when we would visit the grocery store together and he would ask to have the sugary candy that was intentionally put on his eye level or the cereal that had nothing but colorful shapes and animal characters on the outside of the box. When the answer was no, he would propel himself on the floor as if he were experiencing some uncontrollable spasm that took over his body. He was unable to control the feeling. His anger fit would continue until his face turned bright red and he had attracted attention from all the mothers shopping with their well-behaved angelic children. Eventually when nothing else was working and most of the patrons had cleared the store, I would gently suggest he pull out his imaginary dandelion and begin blowing the flowers. This gentle tool helped him calm the blaze inside of his sweet little body.

Ask your child to gently close their eyes and begin focusing on their breath. As they begin to settle in and relax, take them on an imaginary journey into a beautiful wide-open field. You can use your imagination and create a peaceful scene for them. I used to remind my son of the wind that was gently blowing, and all the colorful flowers seemed to dance to the melody of the blowing air. I even included a gentle flowing stream nestled in a wooded glen. Try to be as descriptive as possible. Allow them to see themselves picking a dandelion flower from the earth, gently clipping the stem, careful to not break the shaft. Invite them to raise the dandelion flower to their mouth and exhale the white fluffy flowers into the wind. Stay with them as you encourage them to watch the fluffy blooms float away until they can't see them anymore. Remind them to check into themselves and feel how differently their body feels after blowing the magic dandelion flowers. This is a beautiful technique to use even when we are not feeling that tsunami of emotion.

Numbering - To Help Navigate Fear

Sometimes when we feel a strong energetic charge of fear, we think we need some complicated tool to ease the sensation. Offering to your children the idea of using the simplicity of their breath can help them face their fear. Each emotion has a different charge, fear included.

I used this tool with my oldest son when he entered his first day of kindergarten. I drove him to the very first day. He was about to explore his life without me. Julian was a very shy little boy, terrified of being without me by his side. I began teaching him this technique when I witnessed him crying whenever we were separated.

As we drove together toward his school for the first time in our large, black SUV, I can remember watching him in the rear-view mirror begin to feel the fear. As he sat quietly in his booster seat staring out of the window, to my delight, he began practicing what I called numbering. Inhale five breaths, hold for five, then exhale slowly for five. Over and over, I saw him practice his breathing. As we approached the sharp turn into the driveway of Harford Day School, I remember noticing a calmness when Julian allowed the new teacher to open the car door and welcome him into the special building for the kindergarteners. I, on the other hand, experienced a waterfall of tears as I pulled away, leaving my firstborn on his first day of the rest of his life.

Have your child first quietly nestle into themselves. Invite them to sit in that comfortable position either sitting up straight or lying down. Comfort is queen when we are in mindful awareness. Have them think of whatever scenario that is causing the fear in their bodies. Invite them to breathe it in rather than push it away. Teaching them to have a friendly relationship with fear can help them not be stuck in it. If they were being chased by a large furry bear, fear would be rational. Irrational fear is an illusion that doesn't exist. If we understand the two, we can help the younger generation understand the same. There is nothing on the other side of irrational fear.

Once they are noticing a calmer energy within themselves, have them begin counting and breathing at the same time. As they breathe in, count to five. Have them hold it at the top for five counts, then slowly exhale for another five counts. Repeat this pattern until the fear energy has subsided. Whether your child is trying something new, like jumping off a high dive for the first time or taking a spelling test, calming in a place of tranquility will allow them to enjoy the process and to improve their experience. You can offer this technique to your inner child to help calm yourself when faced with a challenging situation.

Snow-Globing - To Help Navigate Anxiety

Do you ever feel there are so many thoughts in your mind that you can't think straight? Do you ever wake up in the middle of the night flooded with an avalanche of thought?

This is what I call "snow globing," which represents the energy of stress and anxiety. What really is the emotion of stress? The mind creates so many thoughts, it prevents us from seeing reality. Thoughts are not reality when they cause us to swirl. When we become reactive to something that is not real, it creates the emotion within.

Teaching your children to make decisions from a place of inner calm will help them connect to their truth. The snow globe tool will help them to do just that.

My daughter used to collect snow globes when we would travel. In every gift shop we visited, we would leave with some sort of snow globe that represented the country we were vacationing in—from a scene of kangaroos to those palatial landscapes depicted on a page in a photojournalism book. The idea came to me when she would experience severe anxiety. Whether it be taking a spelling test or going to a friend's house for the first time, a snow globe would be tucked in her pocket. Whenever she felt anxiety or stress bubble up, she would begin shaking the globe and focus on the snow settling to the bottom. The focus on something other than what she was feeling helped her lessen the anxiety and feel more present in reality. Stress is just perception. It is not real.

Not only did I use this tool with my daughter, but I have also offered it to many of my clients. One client in particular felt a sense of anxiety and stress in her workplace. There were some coworkers who caused her to react with old patterns. Even before she entered her workplace each morning, she could feel the stress energy bubble up as she made the daily commute to her job.

"Is there really stress or is it your perception?" I would ask her. We get to understand that our perception creates the emotion our body feels. I suggested, after many weeks of work, that she begin implementing a tool to relieve her anxiety. Her small snow globe with the white snowman inside that had been sitting on a shelf from a trip she made years ago, fit perfectly into her blue linen blazer. Whenever she heard the coworker's voice approaching her desk cubicle, she would begin shaking the globe. She noticed that because she focused on something other than the anxious thoughts, the trigger seemed to disappear. She continues to use it to this day.

I invite you to visit your local dollar store and purchase a small snow globe. Teach your child to first recognize the emotion, locate it in her/his body, and then begin having them shake the globe, breathing and focusing on the snow falling inside. Keep shaking, breathing, and focusing until you and they feel that energetic shift.

Heart-Stoning - To Help Navigate Feeling Alone

This is one of my favorite tools I personally use when I want to feel more grounded and secure. The magic simplicity of nature can connect us to the root of who we are. In chapter four, I offered some information about chakras or energy centers. If you can recall, the first chakra is our root energy center that represents our foundation of who we are. This energy center is connected to the earth when we are in complete balance. Grounding ourselves and our children to nature can help us and them feel this connection. We can experience this in two different ways.

I coined the phrase *heartstoning* after my experience with my mystic healer in Big Sur, California. During the height of COVID, the only activity available to me was going out barefoot into the vastness of nature and collecting heart-shaped rocks from the beach surf. The choices were unlimited, and I was able to find *heartstones* even as large as twelve pounds. This became a bit of an issue when trying to return back to the East Coast. I tried to bring them aboard as my carry on. The entire TSA (Transportation Security Administration) that worked at the small airport in Monterey gathered to examine this unusual object this strange woman with beaded necklaces and long locks of unbrushed blonde hair was trying to carry on. I tried to explain why I wanted to take them home with me. I mentioned they were filled with magic energetic powers from Mother Earth. This comment was not received in the way that I imagined. It was as if I were speaking a foreign language that no one understood. After being told my stones could be dangerous to the pilot, I was allowed to put them into my checked bags. As I put my suitcases that I lived out of for the past five months on the scale, I quickly inhaled in astonishment as the red needle quickly turned to seventy-five pounds. Oops!

Heartstoning helps me connect with the natural energy of love. The stones are reminder that we are always love. To this day at the beaches of Delaware, hiking the mountains in Sedona, or strolling in the untouched ocean waters in Puerto Rico, I *heartstone* with Mother Nature and feel the connection and fullness within me. Have children play a game of who can find the most stones that are shaped like hearts. Let them use their imagination when collecting. What they imagine a heart looks like could be totally different than yours. The idea is for them to bring their focus onto the task at hand and be in unison with Mother Earth. They won't even know it's happening.

Another way for you and your children to feel fulfilled and connected while heartstoning, *is to take a step outside without any shoes on, if weather permits.* I can remember my youngest son always played outside without shoes on, even when the weather turned cold. This was much to the dismay of the generation that believed if children were cold, they would catch their death. I didn't know then that this was one of the most powerful ways my son could connect to himself.

Photographs of Avery were mostly in his birthday suit when he was at the age of self-discovery. I can remember he would get up and sit at the breakfast table in his little underpants, only to race outside to explore with his little brother, Rory. They would spend the day outside playing in the twenty acres of property surrounding our home. It reminded me of little me, when I was his age, playing with my brother and those endless hours outside without a care in the world. To this day Avery never wears shoes. He lives in southern California with his wife, sweet daughter, Ku'uilei, and their dog, Russell.

Earthing or grounding is what I offer my clients as a way to heal their root energy center. When we are connected to ourselves, we are never alone. That energy they begin to feel is rooted into Mother Earth, and that root is also energetically connected to our highest source: God, Universe, Divine, Jesus, Buddha. The beginning phase of healing is with the root chakra. Remembering that the root energy center represents our foundation, if this chakra is out of alignment, it tends to misalign the other six energy centers. At one of my recent retreats in Sedona, my guests practiced earthing each morning. In the chilly air of the Arizona mornings, this practice helped start their mornings the way they wanted to live the rest of their day.

The tools we allow ourselves to practice each day in our healing journey can be the change to heal the collective world. It all begins with you!

Chapter 10

On the Other Side

I can't believe I am here with you in the last pages of my beloved book. It feels as if I have given birth to another baby! My sincere hope is that you understand yourself better. You feel a sense of relief that you can do something about those uncontrolled and uncomfortable emotions. There is support all around you to shift yourself into a place of inner happiness and joy. We are all in this game of life-healing together.

I will recap some of the tools I offered throughout the book so you can choose one or many at a glance. Remember, the magic is when you take the first small step forward. Here is a quick glance at my healing tools:

Meditation, Meditation, Meditation

When we begin our healing process, we must do this in a quiet head-space in order to recognize the thoughts in which we have been identifying.

Be Present to the Sensation

Remember, our bodies hold the answers to what needs to be healed and where. Those energy centers from your root chakra to the crown of your head are where the energy of your stories show up. Begin staying present to which energy center is speaking to you.

Reparenting That Inner Child

The little one inside of you has been waiting for you. She/he is tired of being the one in charge and feeling all those heavy emotions. You can help her/him merge with the adult in you, so you can be that powerful force together.

Building Your Happily Ever After

You now can rewrite the script of your life. You have cleared that path for this new you to follow. The sky's the limit in what is possible when you have made space for how you want to live and what you want to experience.

Break the Cycle

It all begins with you. If you are living in old patterns, it is possible, with guidance, to change what no longer serves you. Break that pattern and you will feel the abundance that has been waiting for you.

From using these practices and tools in this book, my clients have shifted from where they thought they were stuck with no way out of thinking small, not feeling enough, not deserving to live in abundance, and settling for mediocrity. They have all worked hard to heal their inner foundation, change their limited thoughts and beliefs, and vibrate from a new and empowering frequency. It all began with them. I was just their guide. I continue to remind those I have the pleasure to work with, that all that they seek is already within them. They get to chip away the layers in which they negatively identify. Just remember, healing is a lifelong process. We commit to healing the layers that are as thick as a rose petal, and we commit to healing the layers that sit as deep as a dandelion weed.

The following magic of healing comes from my *No Matter What Women/ Men* whom I have worked with in the past, and some I continue to work with to this day. I define a *NMWM* as an empowered person. who never listens to their own excuses to not change, who seeks accountability whenever possible, so they don't journey alone, who believes in new possibilities and never loses hope in themselves.

The Magic

Before the work, Beth was feeling low-energy, filled with resentment and anger toward her past. She was putting her family's needs before her own and not allowing herself to experience fun, joy, or creativity.

After working with me and practicing the tools in this book, she completely changed her morning ritual. She made a promise to herself that before she helps anyone in her family, she chooses one thing from her *Joy Jar,* whether it be meditation, a quiet walk outside, or a long, hot shower, and takes care of herself first. Her family even knows not to bother her until they hear the neighborhood church bell ring.

Before the work, Samantha was feeling disempowered in her marriage. She realized she was settling for mediocrity and was only staying in it out of the fear of being judged by her children and her friends. She recognized the same patterns were repeating themselves over and over again. Her husband was unwilling to get any help.

After working with me and practicing the tools in this book, Samantha regained her self-confidence, healed her solar plexus chakra, and began to reparent her inner child trauma identity. She now lives a physically and financially independent life full of inner love. Samantha has even been able to develop a friendship with her former husband.

Before the work, Lia was feeling alone and didn't understand why she couldn't find love again after a tumultuous divorce. She was convinced she would never love again.

After working with me and practicing the tools in this book, she began to love herself by loving her inner child. She even felt an energetic shift in her sacral chakra after experiencing my womb meditations. She recently sent me a photograph from Germany where she and her new love were enjoying a romantic dinner together on the banks of the Danube River.

Before the work, Leanne was surrounded by family drama whenever anyone gathered for a visit in her home. There were heated arguments, ruined dinners, and emotional tension.

After working with me and practicing the tools in this book, she has learned to set strong, yet loving boundaries with her entire family. Her home is now the peace sanctuary that sets the tone for her beloved children and grandchildren.

Before the work, Deb had no self-confidence, and her identity was wrapped around caring for her husband who became very ill. She would say to me, "I don't know who I will be without being a caregiver."

After working with me and practicing the tools in this book, she changed her inner narrative, began journaling her daily *Joy List,* and promised herself she would only do the things that lit her up. After the passing of her beloved husband, she now teaches her passion of massage therapy with an online school and writes powerful meditations for the school to use in their curriculum. May I send blessings to her beloved husband. May his passing shine light on his beautiful wife.

Before the work, Susan was experiencing some emotional setbacks after working with me two years prior. After a pelvic injury and the death of her father, she wanted to explore herself in an even deeper way. The emotions of shame, guilt, and resentment from the past had returned. Those old emotions were preventing her from finding a new job.

After working with me and practicing the tools in this book, she began to love that inner little child inside her that used to sit on an old oak tree stump with her stuffed rabbit, hiding from her grandfather. With this new loving energetic confidence, she was hired at her dream job working as a corporate legal counsel in a small town in Holland.

Write a Vow or Promise Letter to Yourself

This is the time . . . the time to take that step . . . the time for you to be impeccable to your word and do what your inner self has longed for you to experience. Heal yourself *no matter what!*

This last tool is something I experienced myself and still have framed and hanging in my office. Write a promissory note to yourself and to that inner little child. Promise that you will take those small steps to get to the other side. Promise yourself that you will be consistent and seek support when you feel you can't experience this journey alone.

> *I_____, do solemnly swear that I will always believe in my inner golden sparkle. I will take the small, but measurable steps with love and kindness. I will reach out for support whenever I feel afraid and don't want to experience this healing work alone. I will meet myself wherever I am and celebrate even the smallest of steps. I will never judge myself or treat my inner child the way my parents treated her/him. I will be patient. I will be kind. I will love every part of me.*
> *I promise YOU.*
> *Signed with pure love, _____*

Thank you from the bottom of my heart for reading my book and believing there is an even greater and more powerful YOU! I cannot wait to meet this new you, and when we meet, we will both celebrate together.

Gratitude

"A rising tide lifts all boats."
—John F. Kennedy

On this journey, I want to acknowledge those people in my life who have lifted me up, believed in me and raised me up to the woman I've become.

There have been so many people who served as my life preserver when my current got too choppy. Thank you for helping weather the storm and allowing me to see my vision with clarity.

I couldn't have experienced this alone.

To all my clients, also known as my #NoMatterWhatWomen, who do whatever it takes to show up for themselves. You inspire me daily.

To my children Julian, Fiona, Avery, and Rory, who continue to believe in who they are and live authentically and boldly. Thank you for being my mirrors.

To my entire family & friends who have been there for me in my past and my present, your continued support means the world to me. You know who you are.

To my writing coach and mentor, Sara Connell (Thought Leader Academy) ~ you have taught me that I am a writer, even when I thought I wasn't. You have shown me how to live a life of creative abundance and prosperity.

To Muse Literary ~ Thank you for your diligence, inspiration and tireless work to bring this book to the world.

To my creative team, Danielle Codere (Free Range Unicorn, LLC) and Hannah Duncan (Hannah Duncan Photography) ~ With your help I was able to put my highest self out into the world.

You have all helped me shine so that I can be a light for others.

I am eternally grateful.

I love you,
Sarah Vie

Afterword

Wow, here we are at the very end of the book! I hope you have deepened the connection to who you are and realized that you are not your pain, you are not your limitations. You are not what happened to you in your past. You are a pure, authentic being who is full of one energy—the energy of love.

I wish I had known many things that I know now, but if I knew them, I wouldn't have become who I am today. Our difficulties can become our growth. There is support and help for everyone to unearth your most beautiful selves.

I wanted to share with you some of my readers' answers to my question, *what would you have wished you had known?*

Here's what they said:

- I wish I had known that I'm perfect because of my imperfections.
- I wish I had known how to trust me and to listen to my intuition.
- I wish I had known that I really did have the strength to make better decisions.
- I wish I had known that I was smart and that I just learn in a different way.
- I wish I had known that my worth isn't determined by the men I attracted.

- I wish I had known that even if you feel like you're the only one who doesn't get something, you're not!
- I wish I had known that I am enough just as I am.
- I wish I had known to love myself more, that I am enough.
- I wish I had known that I could be proud of myself and not seek this approval from others.
- I wish I had known that I wasn't broken and defective.
- I wish I had known I am as strong and beautiful on the outside and just as amazing on the inside.
- I wish I had known that I wasn't alone.
- I wish I had known it's not my responsibility.
- I wish I would have known that some of the small things I worried about really didn't matter.
- I wish I had known it's okay to be broken. I am a work in progress.
- I wish I had known the power of my independence and that it is something not everyone will experience in life.
- I wish I had known that I was valuable and loved.
- I wish I had known that it was something that happened and not a part of who I was.
- I wish I had known to look within rather than externally for love.
- I wish I had known I was worth loving and not stupid.
- I wish I had known not to be in such a hurry; it's okay to take things slow and to think things through.
- I wish I'd known that the most important things in life are not things.
- I wish I had known my purpose is to live from my heart.
- I wish I had known I could do anything and not be afraid.
- I wish I had known that my emotions were valid and my most important allies for growth.
- I wish I had known that asking for help isn't a weakness.

- I wish I had known that resistance to "what is" causes suffering. It is the secret to oneness or okayness.
- I wish I had known that learning and being willing to love myself is the way to let others in to love me, too.
- I wish I had known that when you died you weren't gone, regardless of being raised in the church and told about Heaven.
- I wish I'd known that I was worthy of unconditional love. I'm so lucky to have made that discovery while working with you.
- I wish I had known that I was enough, that I did not have to apologize for being exactly who God intended me to be.
- I wish I had known about the field of potentiality around myself and others.

Let's Talk

Now, I want to hear YOUR answer! Share your *what you wish you had known* below.

About the Author

For the past 10 years, Sarah Vie has been transforming women's lives-including her own. Sarah is a Master at helping amplify financial abundance, career success, love in relationships and health and wellness. She is an internationally sought out energy healer, meditation guide and manifesting mentor, helping women and men live abundant, happy, and peaceful lives.

She has been featured on by ABC, NBC, CBS affiliates. Her articles have been published in *Huffington Post, Modern Mom* magazine and *Thrive Global*. Her beloved and best selling first book, *Let Your Inner Golden Sparkle Shine*, is still guiding children to look within themselves for the answers that they seek.